D0897881

FRONTIER BISHOP

frontier Bishop

**THE LIFE
OF
BISHOP
SIMON BRUTÉ**

by

JAMES ROOSEVELT BAYLEY

First Bishop of Newark

Edited by ALBERT J. NEVINS, M.M.

OUR SUNDAY VISITOR, INC.

Noll Plaza, Huntington, Ind. 46750

NIHIL OBSTAT: Rev. Lawrence Gollner, Censor Librorum.

IMPRIMATUR: ✠Leo A. Pursley, D.D., Bishop of Fort Wayne-South-Bend.

Published and printed and bound in the U.S.A. by
OUR SUNDAY VISITOR, INC.
Noll Plaza, Huntington, Indiana 46750

836

BISHOP SIMON GABRIEL BRUTÉ
First Bishop of Vincennes, Indiana

Engraving by J. A. O'Neill, New York, in Memoirs of the Right Reverend Simon Wm. Gabriel Bruté, D.D., published in New York by D. & J. Sadlier & Co., 1861.

CONTENTS

INTRODUCTION

THERE is no need for these preparatory remarks to amplify the life of Bishop Simon Bruté, a giant of the early American frontier. But something should be said about the author of this biography and how it came to be written.

If there had been a register of New York society in the early nineteenth century, the name of Bayley would have been high on the list. It was a well-to-do colonial name that had given many prominent figures to the burgeoning American life.

James Roosevelt Bayley was born in Rye, Westchester County, New York, on August 23, 1814. On his mother's side he was to be related to Theodore, Eleanor, and more indirectly, Franklin D. Roosevelt. On his father's side, he was a cousin of Elizabeth Bayley Seton, who was to become internationally famous as Mother Seton, the foundress of the Sisters of Charity.

Young Bayley attended Trinity College and went on to Hartford Seminary to prepare himself for the Episcopal ministry. He was ordained for the Episcopal Church in 1835 and was assigned as rector of St. Peter's Church, Harlem, then a pleasant, open place of suburban living. In 1841, Bayley took a trip to Europe which was in intellectual ferment, brought about by the writings of John Henry Newman, who had become the leader and spokesman for the Oxford

Movement, and who at the time was still four years away from being received into the Catholic Church.

One of Newman's works, *Tract XC,* particularly impressed the young Episcopal priest. In this polemic, Newman maintained that the Thirty-Nine Articles of the Church of England were political, rather than religious, and that they rejected papal political supremacy and not religious supremacy. Newman was silenced because of this tract and as a result began his inevitable move to Catholicism. *Tract XC* catalyzed Father Bayley's thinking and led him to examine the credentials of Catholicism.

The following year James Roosevelt Bayley resigned from his Harlem parish and was received into the Catholic Church. Since he had not married, he decided to remain in his career choice. He went to Paris and entered the Seminary of Saint Sulpice, where Bruté had also studied. Two years later (1844) he was ordained a Catholic priest and returned to America where because of his education and culture he was appointed vice-president of Saint John's College, a position he held for the next four years. In 1848 he was named secretary to the then Bishop John Hughes of New York. It was during this period that he came across the Bruté journals and manuscripts and began putting them in order, hoping to publish both a life of Bishop Bruté and an eye-witness account of the terror of the French Revolution.

In 1853, at the age of 39, James Roosevelt Bayley was appointed the first Bishop of Newark (N.J.). That same year saw his first book published, *A History of the Catholic Church in New York City.* Two years later, he completed the French Revolution memoirs of Bishop Bruté which was later published by D. & J. Sadlier & Co. This sketch of Bruté's life was written as an introduction to that volume. Bishop Bayley was transferred to the mother see of the United States, the Archdiocese of Baltimore, in 1872. For the next four years he was the ranking Catholic prelate in the United States. In 1877 (October 3) while in Newark, N.J., he died. He was buried at St. Joseph's Convent, Emmitsburg, Maryland, original foundation of Mother Seton.

Except for some editing to accommodate readability (incorporation of footnotes into the text, archaic spellings, shortening of paragraphs, etc.), the life of Bishop Bruté is exactly as Bishop Bayley wrote it. This sketch of Bishop Bruté is reprinted because of its historical importance and in the hope the reader will be persuaded to read additional literature on Vincennes, Bishop Bruté and his contemporaries, in what was an exciting and magnificent period in American history.

ALBERT J. NEVINS, M.M.
Editor

PREFACE

IT may be proper for me, to state in what manner the following papers came into my possession, and the reasons which have induced me to publish them. In 1847, Monsignor De La Hailandiere, the successor of Bishop Bruté, in the See of Vincennes, presented to the Archbishop (then Bishop) of New York a large number of manuscripts which had belonged to his predecessor.

In examining them, my first idea was, to embody them in a "Life and Times of Bishop Bruté," to contain a contemporaneous history of the Catholic Church in this country, and a selection from his extensive and valuable correspondence. In this view I collected a large number of letters, and documents, and made many notes. But, such an undertaking, as Lord Bacon says of learning, "cometh of opportunity of leisure," and my constant occupations then, and since, have never permitted me to carry out my design.

In preparing this brief sketch of Bishop Bruté's life from the memoranda in my possession, it will be perceived that I have not attempted a biography, properly so called, but have merely drawn out a thread of narrative to string the notes on. It is indeed to be regretted that Bishop Bruté did not write an autobiography. His life until he came to this country, was passed among the most exciting events that ever occurred— he was personally acquainted with a large number of the ac-

13

tors in them—his memory was strong and accurate, and he might have written a book of great historical value. His notes and memoranda show, that at one time he contemplated something of the sort, but on this account they are often less useful to others, being merely hints and memoranda to assist his memory.

"There is no sort of Literature," he writes in a note on 'Spence's Anecdotes,' "which has afforded me more pleasure than biographies and memoirs. I sometimes think of amusing myself by writing an account of my life. There is a quantity of anecdotes and observations which occur to me, and which if they were written down would amuse and interest my associates and friends, and might remain *en depôt* in the library."

In looking over the work, now that it is finished, my only regret is, that the biographical sketch is not more worthy of the holy man, who is the subject of it. Those who knew him, I am afraid, will be particularly disappointed at my poor silhouette likeness of him. But if so, they must distribute the blame among themselves, for some one of them should, long before this, have written a biography of one, whom they remember, and so often speak of, as the model of every ecclesiastical virtue and whose memory for piety and learning is so justly in benediction among them.

CHAPTER I

Family and Birth

SIMON Gabriel Bruté, the subject of this sketch was born in Rennes, the capital of the ancient Province of Brittany, in France, on the night of the 20th of March, 1779, and was baptized early the next morning in the Parish Church of St. Germain.

His father, Simon William Gabriel Bruté de Remur, who belonged to an ancient and very respectable family, was born at Paris in 1729, and was at the time of his son's birth, Superintendent of the Royal Domains in Brittany. His father was twice married. First to Mary Jeanne LeChat, at Paris in 1756, by whom he had seven children; and then to Madame Vatar at Rennes in 1778, by whom he had two children, the subject of this sketch, and his brother Augustine, born in 1789.

His mother, Jeanne Renée Le Saulnier de Vauhelle, born at St. Brieux in 1736, was at the time of her marriage with Mr. Bruté the widow of Francis Vatar, Printer to the King and Parliament at Rennes. "My mother has often told me," says Bruté, "that the Vatars were of English origin; and had pursued the occupation of printing since its invention in the 14th Century. The books printed by Mr. Vatar were chiefly those on the jurisprudence of the province. There were 130,000 francs worth of these books in store when the Constituent Assembly abolished all local laws and customs, and thus entirely destroyed the value of those which my

15

mother, who had inherited the title of Printer to the King and Parliament, had on hand."

In his notes, Bruté writes: "My mother's mother, Claudienne Elienor Robert, died in 1791, aged 81 years. Her brother, my grand uncle, was Peter Robert, Prior of Etables of the Order of Praemonstratentians, who died in 1795 in the Hospital of Guingcamp, prisoner for the Faith."

After Simon's birth, he was sent into the country to a nurse, according to the general custom of those times. "I remained with my nurse fifteen months," he recalls. "She lived at a small village about five miles from Rennes, on the road to Brest. There were three villages or hamlets, one was called Hell, another Paradise, and the third Purgatory. My nurse lived in Hell. She sometimes lent me to another poor woman who used to beg, and made use of my presence on one of her arms to excite compassion. This thought has often afforded me pleasure. I always remained much attached to my nurse; and she used to come and see me sometimes, when I was in the Seminary of Rennes in 1808 and 9."

"My mother," he says in another memoranda, "was a woman of strong mind who understood the world and had great experience in business matters, but always faithful to her religion, hid the priests and assisted them in many different ways, during the Revolution; the respect of all classes of people was a great protection to her and her family in the worst of times."

The Bruté place of residence was in the Palace of Parliament, in which his family, on his mother's side, had occupied apartments in one of the wings since 1660. The position held by his father, as Superintendent of the Finances of the Province, with the anticipation of succeeding to the first Brevet of Farmer-General of the Revenues at Paris, which had been promised to him, seemed to open the most brilliant worldly prospects.

" 'You were born to live in opulence,' my good mother often said to me," Bishop Bruté remarks in one of his notes.

"My earliest recollections," he adds, "are connected with the entertainment given by my father, at his residence in the city, and at his country house in Fricot in the Faubourg St. Helier, to the deputies, the military officers, and the nobles, at the time of the meeting of the *Etats de la Province*. I remember seeing no less than five of our bishops at his table at one time. We children were placed at a little side table, where our pride, and our love for good things, were alike mortified."

"God ordered it otherwise," he goes on to say, alluding to his mother's words, "my father died (27th February, 1786) a few days after a very painful operation which had been rendered necessary by a fall from his horse—and instead of a succession of opulence, left his affairs in the greatest disorder."

" 'Your father,' my mother often said to me, 'could never be made to distrust anyone.' He believed every person to be good and honest like himself—and the state of his accounts at the time of his death showed it, for not only were all his affairs in confusion, but it was found that he had allowed persons to run in debt to him, upwards of a million of francs. The friends of the family, the most eminent lawyers of the city, advised my mother to renounce the succession; but she, very justly, regarded an honorable name as of more importance than wealth, and in order to preserve this to us, she determined to take upon herself the management of his affairs, even at the sacrifice of her own property. She accordingly addressed herself to the task, and with the assistance of two accountants, Messrs. Jourdain and Henaut, for whom she has often charged me to preserve feelings of lively gratitude, she worked day and night until she got my father's accounts in order; and owing to her diligence and management, the losses were much less than they would otherwise have been, and his debts were all paid."

To keep memories alive Bishop Bruté was wont to draw sketches. The above was found among his papers. His notes follow:

"1. The Cathedral—formerly the Abbey Church—St. Melanie, founded by St. Melanie in the 6th century, possessed his reliques, and also those of St. Amand, like him one of the early Bishops of Rennes. I remember seeing the Benedictines there in their habit, and was present several times at the services in 1787-1788, the impression made upon my mind by the majestic simplicity of their ceremonies and the divine chant is still fresh in my mind, and the sound of their voices as they chanted the psalm, 'cum invocarum, etc,' in the office of Complin, still echoes in my ears and in my heart—and then the benediction and the sound of the big bell of the Abbey at that moment. In 1791 the Church and Abbey were usurped by the revolutionary clergy, in 1792 they became the prison of the Catholic clergy, who remained faithful to their vows and would not take the new oath. I visited them twice while they were confined there, disguised as a baker's boy and carrying a big bread basket on my head. In 1793-94 the Church was turned into a stable for the cavalry, in 1795 into the City Hospital, that having been taken possession of for an Arsenal, in 1802 restored to the divine service as the Cathedral of the Diocese.

"2. The Bishop's Residence—a more modern building—the 'pavilion' on the side changed into a Picture Gallery, that on the other into a Botonical School, in 1799, restored to the Bishop in 1802. The Duke of Angouleme lodged there in 1814.

"3. The Gardens of the Eveche, and (4) their extension, forming a beautiful Botonical Garden, opening upon the country towards St. Michael and the magnificent prospect of Belle-vue (6), two miles eastward, and towards St. Lawrence (7) three miles.

"5. The Garden of the Abbey.

"6. The Promenade, called 'Thabor,' belonging to the Abbey, with its superb terraces, made by the Benedictine Novices during their times of recreation. How often have I walked there alone or with my good Mother, the virtuous and charitable house of Montluc-Cice. I visited all these beloved spots in 1815. I have made this sketch and wrote this note during recreation—Evening of Palm Sunday, with little hope of ever seeing them again—Eternity."

CHAPTER II

Early Influences

IT is evident, not only from the circumstances here related, but from her conduct during the Revolution, her letters to her son, the manner in which he always alludes to her in his memoranda and letters to others, that Madame Bruté was a woman of more than ordinary intelligence and strength of character. This was regulated and directed by a fervent and devoted piety. There can be no doubt that, under God, the eminently religious character of her son, which caused, we may say, every thought, word and action of his whole life to be guided by faith, was owing to the instructions and example of his excellent mother.

He was happy also in enjoying, during those tender years, when the character is formed, the guidance of one of the best of priests, the Abbé Carron, so well known for his labors in England, and the admirable books of piety which were written by him.

Guy Touffaint Julien Carron was born at Rennes in 1760. Having distinguished himself by his zeal, and particularly by his charity towards the poor, he was imprisoned in 1792 for refusing to take the civic oath. Exiled the same year, he founded several churches and schools in England. He returned to France in 1814 and died in 1821. He was author of a large number of works of piety. The celebrated Lamennais revered him as a saint. The Baron D'Eckstein, whom he had known intimately, says: "This man had the genius of goodness." In a letter to Bishop Flaget from Mount St. Mary's, dated June 9, 1821, Father Bruté mentions the death of Abbé Carron at Paris: "My first spiritual father—so often called the Saint Vincent de Paul of our days."

"My first Confessor," he says in his notes, "was Mr. Carron, Vicar of the Parish of St. Germain, then a very young priest, but already so remarkable for his exemplary life, and most fervent piety, that he was called 'the Abbé Térèse' in allusion to St. Teresa. This was soon after the death of my father, when I was about eight years old. I remember well that the first time I went to confession to him, he gave me, as I withdrew from his confessional, which stood in the chapel of the Blessed Virgin, a little book in French, entitled 'The Death of Abel.' As I was retiring, he came out of the confessional, and gave me the book. I remember his face, as it appeared at that moment, with such an expression of amiability and piety upon it. I was his penitent for several years, until 1791, the last year of the free exercise of religion in France, during which year I had the happiness of making my first communion. I went regularly to confession, but up to that time, thanks be to God, my excellent mother, and I must add excellent teachers, I had little to confess. Although I had attended public schools four or five years, I was an entire stranger to all improper notions—and my chief matter of reproach, at the time of making my general confession for first communion, was the having taken an apple from the stand of an old fruit-woman.

"During the same interval, I learned my catechism at school, though at times I attended the public catechism at the parish church, to recite portions of the Holy Scripture, which we learned by heart. I remember that, on one occasion, having repeated the history of the sacrifice of Abraham, I obtained as a reward, quite a large print of the Annunciation pasted on a board with a margin of gilt paper around it. It hung for long years by the side of my bed, and I can still call to mind the strange, vivid associations of the Blessed Virgin and good Father Carron, in my childish impressions of piety and holiness of life. My first prayer book also made a great impression on my mind. It was a 'Paroissien,' bound in green morocco with gilt edges, and was given to me on the very day of my father's funeral, February 28, 1786. I had long desired to have one, and I presume that there was not a little vanity mixed up with the devotion with which I followed the Mass and Office in my beautiful prayer book, at the college, and the parish church. I had it in my possession twenty years afterwards, with its broken covers, defaced binding, and some torn leaves, but lost it somehow or other in my many journeyings.

"I made my first Communion, as I have said, in 1791. There were about 200 of us, of the first or second communion, for it was the excellent custom of those times, to make the second communion with the same preparation as the first, after a short spiritual retreat. I thank thee, oh! my God, for the state of innocence and piety I was in the day I performed this most important act."

The place in which this retreat for first Communion was conducted, seems to have been a very strange one. From an allusion to it, in one of his memoranda, I would infer, that it was what might be called the Hall of the Charnel-House of the cemetery near the church. He speaks of it as "a long, narrow room filled with benches, with the skulls and bones of many generations of those who had preceded them, piled according to the custom of our cemeteries, in a sort of upper story over our heads, so that we could see them through the lattice work which surrounded them. This sight made us very serious and devout, especially on the first day of the retreat. I do not remember anything in particular in regard to the instructions that were addressed to us, except that they were as usual, on sin, death, judgment, the divine Sacrament, the happiness of serving God—and that they made upon us the impressions they were intended to produce. I walked among the tombs during the intervals with some of my companions, and I remember that we were very much in earnest, and animated one another by our remarks, and by our expressions of respect toward the good priests who conducted our retreat, especially Mr. Carron and Mr. Desbouillon—this last a saint of goodness, and penance, and zeal, and charity toward the poor, and heavenly preaching—but a small, ugly, odd looking man, so that some of us burst out into a laugh at a curious comparison which he made, and the strange gesticulation by which it was accompanied. Oh! how sorry we were, and when the instruction was over, we went to him and asked his pardon, which he so kindly and cheerfully gave us. He is dead long since, and I have no doubt a saint in heaven. Whilst other particulars have vanished, the general impression it made is still strong on my memory.

"I remember however the many sittings by the confessional of Mr. Carron, in the Chapel of the Blessed Virgin, in our huge Gothic Church of St. Germain; the small statue of our Blessed Mother, in a white and blue mantle on the altar —and the last evening when I received absolution; the effort to make a good act of contrition, and the earnest desire for a good communion, a good death, and heaven—and then going to say the 'Miserere' on my knees, on a huge tomb near the high altar, where we were to receive our Lord the next morning. The events of the next day, it would indeed be hard to forget; the early rising, the prayer for the soul of my dear departed father—the benediction asked from my mother on my knees—the spirit of recollection and devotion which I cherished, in view of the important act I was about to perform; somewhat disturbed by the anxiety of our good Mr. Leblanc, in regard to my dress and 'frisure,' and the huge candle I was to carry. I remember singing the Canticle of Fenelon, *'Mon bien aimé ne paroit pas encore'*—the departure for church—seeing our friends coming from all sides—the entrance of the church—all seated in rows so near one another, yet such good order and silence—so much fervour in singing the canticles—such an indescribable suspense and delight of the heart until the moment should come to receive; but before doing so, reciting in front of all, the Act of Consecration, with Térèsè Champion for my companion, as the representative of the girls. Twenty years afterwards when I returned to France, I found her, still so faithful in her perseverance, so devoted to our blessed Lord. It seems strange to me now, that all distinct remembrance of the act itself is lost. I am sure it was all faith, and pure desire of union with God, and of the thanksgiving afterwards, I only remember the sincerity and ardor of the offerings . . . the return home, with poor Lamiral, the lad put to the charge of my mother, who for many years after that until he had got his trade, fulfilled towards him the happy duty, imposed that day, upon all the young communicants, belonging to the more respectable families, of choosing from amongst the poor, a 'brother of Communion' to be taken care of and brought up as a member of the family. My heart is full, when I think of that day —thanks! thanks oh my God."

The above memoranda show how lively were Bishop Bruté's recollections of the events and persons of his youth. His papers afford abundant evidence how closely his heart clung at all periods of his life, to the memory of his native city and province. Sometimes it is a little sketch of a building, or church, within the city, or in the suburbs, done with his pen, with a few words of affectionate remembrance, or some circumstance which occurred there, written under it. Sometimes a fuller description, recalling the ancient religious glories of his much loved Brittany and his own recollections of the place and the persons who dwelt on the spot described in his time. It is to be regretted that his memoranda upon these subjects, are of so fragmentary a nature—being generally merely hints, or words to assist his memory, rather than detailed descriptions, which would now be so interesting. From one of these pages of jottings, as they may be called, it appears that at the time of his father's death in 1786, he was at a boarding school, kept by Madame Badier, in the Parish of All Saints, which was as he mentions one of the largest parishes in Rennes. He alludes to the narrow street, opposite the church, through which they were accustomed to pass, when they took their promenade on Wednesday of each week, the Church itself, the entrance, the high altar, the "Eternal Father" over it, the chapel of Mr. Rebulet, the processions of

Corpus Christi and the Assumption with the grand statue of the Blessed Virgin, of Palm Sunday, and so on.

In a note he speaks of a mason who was killed in a fall in 1794, when attempting to pull down the "Eternal Father." The church was burnt this year (1794) with forty houses; the ruins were afterwards removed and the spot left open.

He adds, "I note down these remembrances in 1821, on the Feast of All Saints, 34 years after; everything is still fresh in my mind and present to me; I could describe everything—the street—the signs over the shops—the shops themselves—the fruit stalls—the bells on the Vigils of the Feasts—the Glas (the passing-bell for the dead) during the whole evening before the Feast of All Saints." In a memorandum headed: "Places where I have studied"—which from its minute details, seems to have been written as an exercise of local memory, it appears that his first school where he learned to read, was kept by a certain Mademoiselle Rosé in the "Rue aux Foulons" and that the "Pension" of Madame Badier, above alluded to, was his second school. With his lively imagination, tenacious memory and excellent disposition he must have been an apt scholar from the beginning and seems to have won the affections alike of his teachers and fellow students. He attended the college at Rennes from 1788 to 1791, under the particular supervision of Father Sorette, of whom he has left a touching account.

CHAPTER III

Death of Abbé Sorette

AMONG Bishop Bruté's papers are many vignettes of the French Revolution. One concerns Abbé Sorette, his teacher and friend: "The Abbé Sorette was a young priest, not yet thirty years of age, when he was appointed professor at the College of Rennes, the first year of the French Revolution. I studied under him, and became very much attached to him, and he took a particular interest in me, and sometimes did my mother the honor to come and dine with us. The charming modesty, candor, piety, and yet sprightliness and gaiety of that most excellent man, endeared him to all who knew him.

"When the Revolutionary oaths were imposed upon the clergy, he refused to take them, and being expelled in consequence from the college, he retired to the country parish of Le Chatellier near Parigné, 16 or 18 miles from Rennes. It was here he had been stationed by the bishop when first ordained, and during the few years of his ministry, had won the unbounded affection of his own, and all the neighboring parishes. 'Mr. Sorette'! with what an accent of affection was that name pronounced by every one, before his death, and many years afterwards. At Le Chatellier, he exercised the duties of his holy ministry, during the worst times of the Revolution, with an undaunted zeal, surrounded in the vicinity, by many other priests of the same fearless, unreserved devotedness; some of whom were, like himself, amongst the victims which the Diocese of Rennes offered to God for the cruel sins and horrid excesses of the times.

"He indeed escaped during the whole reign of Robespierre, and until the laws of death were repealed. Banishment to French Guiana for the younger priests, perpetual imprisonment for the older ones, were the milder orders of the day.

"The more zealous Jacobins, however, were much displeased at this relaxation of the law, and often eluded it. When they discovered any priests in the country, they would often deliberately put them to death on the spot, rather than bring them to the city and deliver them up to the authorities. This was the fate of my dear and respected professor.

"Mr. Sorette led a life of continual alarm and danger, yet of untiring zeal in the fulfillment of his duties. To be finally spent by the sacrifice of his life, after so hard and faithful a service, during his many years of concealment in his own parish and the neighboring parts, was to him an inevitable conclusion of his work. Such were the sentiments he expressed to me, with much fervor and alacrity of mind, two or three weeks before his death.

"He had, at that time, come to our city on his way to the mineral waters of Guichen. He had been advised to go there for a double purpose—to repair his health, which was much shattered by labor and exposure, and to escape for a while from the search made for his apprehension in his own part of the country. He was concealed in the suburb St. Martin at the chateau of the Ladies De Leon, and while there sent word to my mother to let me come and see him. My mother gave me the most earnest charge to persuade him not to venture to Guichen, but to come to our houses and be secreted, where he could be nursed and well taken care of.

"I hurried to him, with most pleasing hopes, to have under our roof my beloved preceptor—and so good a priest— but they were in vain! I arrived at the place, was very cautiously admitted, and enjoyed a most agreeable interview with him. He related to me many of his wonderful escapes. But when I had easily made out to prove to him that it would be very unsafe for him to take up his residence near the waters of Guichen, the conclusion he drew was that he was not so ill as his physicians thought, and that the best thing he could do was to return to his poor people and remain with them to the last. No arguments, no entreaties, could make him accede to the wishes of his friends at Rennes. Two or three days later he returned to Le Chatellier. I never heard directly from him again.

"About three weeks after he had returned to his mission, we received the following information in regard to his end. Poor M. Sorette was called the other day (December 15, 1798) to administer the last sacrament to an old woman, in a little farm house. He had finished and was coming back to his hiding place when a party of Contre-Chouans, who were patrolling the country in search of victims, and who knew that M. Sorette was concealed somewhere in that vicinity, asked a peasant girl whom they met, if she could tell them where they would find the priest, as they needed his services for a sick person. It so happened that she had met M. Sorette but a few moments before, and deceived by their disguise, and supposing them to be friends, she said to them, after a moment's hesitation, 'M. Sorette has left that house yonder, but a minute since, and is passing along the hedge there by the meadow.'

"They immediately ran after him, and as soon as they drew near, fired their guns at him and broke his arm. He immediately stopped and surrendered, and then told them to lead him to the city. But they, knowing that he would only be exiled to Guyenne, told him that they had resolved to put him to death. M. Sorette then entreated them to allow him a few minutes to prepare himself for death. He then knelt down in the grass, and when they had waited a few moments, they shot him on the spot."

CHAPTER IV

The French Revolution

DURING this year (1791), in which, as we have seen, he made his first communion, the Legislative Assembly passed the most severe laws against all the clergy who refused to take the oath to the "Civil Constitution of the Clergy," and as almost all refused to do so, the open and public exercise of religion may be said to have ceased in France.

Previously, the Constituent Assembly, having confiscated all ecclesiastical property on November 4, 1789, and suppressed all religious orders and congregations on March 19, 1790, proceeded on August 24, 1790, in its work of "decatholicising" France by enacting the famous "Civil Constitution of the Clergy," which virtually abrogated the Catholic Church in that country, so far as it was in the power of man to do it. By this infamous law, the State assumed to itself the power of conferring ecclesiastical jurisdiction; the bishops and parish priests were to be chosen by the electors, in the same manner as the assembly; they were forbidden to write to the pope for confirmation.

As soon as it became a law, the most violent measures were instituted to oblige the bishops and clergy to take the oath to it. Out of 135 archbishops and bishops in France, four only took it. The great majority of the clergy also refused to take it. The Civil Constitution is now remembered only as a specimen of the folly of those days and a lesson for

the future, if men ever learn anything from such lessons, which is doubtful.

The college at Rennes was broken up, and from this
time Simon Bruté pursued his studies under private teachers.
In the list of "places where I have studied" he put down
"four years under Mr. Muriel." During these days of persecution (1791-96) he seems to have remained most of the
time at Rennes, in his mother's residence but portions of it
were spent at La Chapelle Bouexie where his half sister, Madame Janisons, resided.

Among his "Notes on the French Revolution" I find en-
dorsed on the back of a letter received by him in 1796, from
the Abbé Després, the following note: "This letter is from M.
Després, then in prison at Vannes. He had been a long time
in concealment at Rennes, and I studied my philosophy under
him." These "Notes" show how great an interest he took in
those holy confessors who at that time suffered and died with
such heroic constancy. Afterwards when they were confined
in prison instead of being immediately condemned to the guillotine, he seized upon every opportunity of visiting them in
disguise to carry them the Blessed Sacrament. He mentions
that as a boy he would go and enter into conversation with
the guards, so as to become known to them and get opportunities of visiting the prisoners, with letters for them concealed in his clothes and sometimes the Blessed Sacrament on
his bosom, followed by a priest in disguise.

The "Notes," short and imperfect, as they are, convey to
the reader, some idea of his manner of life, during that dreadful period. Amidst all its alarms and sufferings, his memoranda show that he was exact and regular in the employment
of his time. He rose early, and no doubt found in those studies, of which he was always so fond, some relief from the
anxieties, which in those days of terror must have disturbed
the most fearless and best regulated minds.

CHAPTER V

Early Rising

T HE following, written on a loose sheet of paper, was among Bishop Bruté's effects. He followed its advice to the end of his life.

"Today I received a letter from my mother dated the 2nd of January, 1819. She was born in 1736, and is consequently in her 84th year. 'My health is very good,' she writes, 'no pains—sleep soundly.' She used to consider early rising, to which she was always accustomed, a pledge of longevity. 'No longevity, my son,' she would say to me, 'except for those who rise early.' She regarded it from a higher point of view, than the mere enjoyment of health, and the prolongation of life. Early rising, she would say, is absolutely necessary for anyone who would faithfully discharge his duties in life; it secures health, gives clearness and soundness to the head, calmness to the mind, freshness to the thoughts and affections, is favorable to pious dispositions, and affords leisure for recollection and meditation, so as to begin the day well, before the hurry of more advanced hours surrounds us with the labors and distractions of common life. And my good mother was right. There is no indulgence to more carefully be guarded against than that of lying abed in the morning. Six hours of sleep is enough alike for old age and youth (childhood requiring more), according to the apothegm of the Salernian school—seven we grant to the lazy, eight to nobody.

"Early rising affords to the virtuous soul the most favorable opportunity of exerting her empire over the body—for, so great is its fondness for rest and indulgence—so strong an effort does it require to break the pleasing chains of sloth and to give up to the easy bed and the quietude of its slumbers always the more agreeable towards morning. It requires each morning a true act of fortitude and self-denial to rise at the appointed time. It is almost the only task that habit does not make easier. My mother enforced this duty, which brings so many precious advantages with it, with the anxious firmness of true love.

"When the poor boy of 12 hesitated to jump out of his bed at 4 or 4½ o'c. in summer, or 5 or 5½ in winter, stretching out his arms, rubbing his eyes, and fighting pitifully at the sound of his mother's voice, 'Gabriel! Gabriel! Get up!' Oh! my mother, how can I ever sufficiently thank you for all your considerate kindness—ever anxious to form your children to habits of virtue and self-denial."

CHAPTER VI

The Revolution Wanes

HE acquired in boyhood and youth," says Father John
McCaffrey, President of Mount St. Mary's College in a Discourse there in 1839, "habits of study, of close and patient
mental application which he retained through life. In spite of
that modesty which prevented him from ever speaking in his
own praise, I could learn from a long and intimate acquaintance with him, and from the testimony of others, that, in the
public schools of his native city, he was distinguished, and
eminently successful. His after life proved it. His mind was
too rich in treasures of classic lore, too amply furnished from
the armories of science, for him to have been a dull or care-
less student. Whether he conversed with a friend or lectured a
class, or heralded the message of salvation from a pulpit, the
evidences of profound knowledge as well as of remarkable
genius incessantly flashed before you. Whatever he once read,
or studied, he remembered. Even in the last years of his life,
when his attention seemed to be absorbed in theology, and
other branches of ecclesiastical learning, he recited with ease
all the Fables of La Fontaine, entire scenes of Racine, Cor-
neille, and the finest passages of the other French writers, or
of the Latin poets. Though less familiar with the Greek clas-
sics, he had read them with advantage, as well as pleasure,
and turned to good account his knowledge of their language,
in the study of the Greek Fathers of the Church.

33

"1. The tribunal represented in the drawing, before which M. Raoul and the Sisters were tried, if we may use such an expression, was the Regular Criminal Court. There were besides, as I have mentioned, two other Tribunals of Death in our poor city of Rennes—one, the Military Commission, presided over by Morin and the Revolutionary Tribunal, under the presidency of Brutus Magnier. Morin and Magnier were strangers to our city."—Note by Bishop Bruté.

"At one time he had in view to enter the French Polytechnic school, and for this reason, he pursued a very extensive course of mathematical science. Subsequently he had the best opportunities in the medical school of Paris, of penetrating deeply into the mysteries of chemistry and natural philosophy. He improved them with his usual diligence. While he devoted himself to severer studies, he gave some share of attention to music and drawing; and in the latter of these accomplishments he attained a proficiency, which in after years was a source of pleasure and advantage to himself, and a means, which he often happily employed, for the purpose of interesting and instructing others. His studies were interrupted by the revolutionary troubles, and he spent about two years in his mother's printing establishment, during which he learned and practiced the business of a compositor. It would appear that he was led to this much less by inclination, than by the reverses which his family had sustained, and the dangers of the times."

This admirable sketch of Bishop Bruté's intellectual character and application, is fully confirmed by his note books, and manuscripts in my possession. I found on the back of a sheet on which he had written some remarks about the art of printing, the following note:

"In 1793-4, during the height of the Terror, my mother made me work in the printing office to save me being enrolled in a regiment made up of children, named 'The Hope of the Country,' and a hopeful set they were. They requested and obtained permission to take part in the 'fusillades' which they often did. When the deputation, whom they sent to request this permission, presented itself before the revolutionary tribunal, they were requested to take their seat alongside of the judges, and preside at the condemnation of some victims, who were handed over to these young scoundrels to be shot. This regiment was formed of boys, of 14, 15 and 16 years of age. My mother was much pressed to allow me to join them and was terribly alarmed on this account. I remained in the printing office for nearly a year, and became a pretty good compositor." He began very early in life, to keep a journal, or as it may more properly be called, a note book. The earliest ones are lost, having probably been destroyed by himself for fear that they would be found by the gendarmes, in some of their domiciliary visits, which were so frequent during those times. The earliest memoranda which I find amongst his papers, are upon some loose leaves, which have been evidently torn from a book of this sort. They are dated in 1795, when the storm of violent persecution had somewhat abated. These memoranda are very brief, and imperfect, and throw little light upon his own personal history, though they would afford no doubt much that would be interesting to a native of Rennes, or a local historian of that part of Brittany. Their chief interest to us consists in the manner in which they mark the gradual change of feeling amongst the people, and the reaction against the Revolution on account of the atrocities which had been committed in its name, and under its influence. The notes contain one anecdote which is appropriate to close discussion of the Revolution.

"After the Terror of 1793," he writes, "the priests who had prevaricated and taken the guilty oaths often made their retraction and did public penance, many with marks of lively sorrow for their scandals. One of them at Grenoble did it with such a degree of compunction that after having spoken a while with increasing fervour, he actually yielded to his grief and died in the pulpit in that act of his exemplary penance."

CHAPTER VII

The Medical Student

ON the 10th of February, 1796, Simon Bruté began the study of medicine with Doctor Duval, an eminent surgeon at Rennes. His copious memoranda of subjects studied, operations assisted at and performed, show with what earnestness he pursued them, and how soon he became skillful himself. He makes no allusion to the motives which caused him to choose this profession—but we may not doubt from his whole character that it was not so much any peculiar attraction which he had for it, as because it would afford him an opportunity of being useful to his fellow creatures. Thoroughly imbued as his heart and soul were with attachment to his religion, there is no evidence that at this time it had entered into his mind to devote himself to the ecclesiastical state—or if he did, the continued persecution directed against anything connected with religion, rendered any such aspirations apparently hopeless. His earnest application to his medical studies did not however in any manner impair his attachment to his faith, or his interest in everything and every person connected with it. Amongst his papers are notes and letters written to him by priests in confinement at Rennes, and elsewhere, thanking him for his words and acts of sympathy and kindness.

Bruté was at this time a member of the society formed by the saintly Abbé Delpuits, ex-Jesuit, who preserved so many youths from the evil principles of the day, and brought back large numbers to a sense of religious duty, by gathering them into a religious confraternity, similar to those established by the Society of Jesus. In a letter to Bishop Flaget, dated April 14, 1812, from Baltimore, he says: "Mr. Delpuits, our good Father of the congregation is dead, pray for him. It is to him I owe my preservation at Paris, my entry into the seminary, and consequently my coming here." In the same letter he gives details of the closing of the minor seminary at Rennes, of the Trappists having been driven away from the "Forests of Camaldules," and of sixty workmen having been sent at three o'clock in the morning to break to pieces the crucifixes and destroy the stations of the cross on Mount Valerien (near Paris) which had recently been restored.

After having pursued his studies for two years, under Doctor Duval he went to Paris, in 1799, to continue them in the medical school there. There he of course enjoyed every advantage in the way of instruction. He attended the lectures of Pinel, Esquirol, Fourcroy, Bichât, and other eminent professors, and according to his custom made notes of all that he heard, which was likely to be useful. Many of these distinguished men were avowed advocates of the prevailing infidelity, and took advantage of every occasion to sneer at religion, and inculcate their false principles. His early religious training, which had preserved his faith and morals during all the horrors and privations of the Revolution, stood him in stead, at this time, and rendered him proof against the sophistries and ridicule to which he was now exposed. Not satisfied however with practicing and openly professing his religion, he entered into a combination with several of his fellow students, particularly those from his own province, boldly to oppose the false principles to which they were obliged to listen. They chose such subjects for their theses, before the class, as enabled them to avow their belief in revelation, and to defend its truth. One of the beneficial effects which followed from this course was that the attention of the government was called to the subject. Bonaparte, then First Consul, was laboring to restore Christianity in France, as the necessary means of reorganizing society; and the infidel professors were made to confine their teaching to its proper limits.

An incident occurred while he was a student of medicine, which illustrates his fidelity to his friends and his earnest fearlessness of character. One of his fellow students, named Collin, a Breton, had been called upon to attend a conspirator who had been wounded by the explosion of the Infernal Machine (December 24, 1800), which had been intended to kill Napoleon Bonaparte, and neglected to give information to the police. For this he was arrested, tried, and confined to prison. Bruté had in vain made every exertion to obtain his liberation and finally, when he was a student at Saint Sulpice and was appointed to serve Cardinal Fesch's Mass at the Tuilleries, took the bold expedient of presenting a petition in favor of his friend to the Emperor in person. He seized the moment when Napoleon was leaving the chapel and ran forward to put the petition in his hand. Bonaparte, absorbed in thought, moved too quickly for him and did not see him— luckily—for he ran the risk of being shot dead as an assassin. He afterwards succeeded in having his friend's sentence commuted into exile to the island of Mauritius. "I went security for him," he says simply. The petition to "Bonaparte, Premier Consul," in favor of his friend, is among the bishop's papers. Bishop Bruté adds, "I never for a single moment had anything to do with any political movements. I came to this country in 1810 and returned to France twice, in 1815 and 1824, but without having seen one of the Bourbons, or received any favors at their hands."

He graduated at the Medical School in 1803 with the highest honors. There were at that time eleven hundred students attending the course; out of these one hundred and twenty were chosen by "concursus" as the best—and amongst this number, Simon Bruté received the first prize, after another examination. He was immediately appointed Physician to the 1st Dispensary in Paris, but having already determined on the day before to study for the Church, he refused it, and afterwards entered the Seminary of St. Sulpice. He was not led to abandon a profession to which he had devoted so many years of assiduous study, and which opened its most brilliant prospects before him, as Dr. McCaffrey remarks, "from any feelings of disgust. He always honored it, as one of the noblest to which a highly gifted and philanthropic man can devote himself. Delightful as his conversation was to all, and to men of science in particular, it was peculiarly so to the student, or to the practitioner and professor of medicine. They often expressed their astonishment, that after a lapse of twenty or thirty years, engrossed by pursuits of a very different order, he retained so perfect and minute a knowledge of all that he had studied in his youth, under the great masters of the French capital."

Bishop Bruté is not recorded as having practiced medicine in the United States, except on one occasion at Mount St. Mary's, when a student having broken his arm, and the doctor was not at hand, he set the broken bone, "most skillfully," as the doctor said when he finally arrived.

CHAPTER VIII

The Seminarian

IN mid-November, 1803, with his mother's blessing and in the company of his brother Augustine, Simon journeyed to Paris to begin private seminary lessons. In October of the following year he entered St. Sulpice Seminary. He turned from medicine only because he had higher and more important objects in view. His eleven hundred classmates in medicine told him that it was easy to find physicians for the body—but the Revolution had made it more difficult to find physicians for the souls of men. For ten years, the houses of religious education and seminaries had been shut up. The guillotine and prisons and exile had spared but a comparatively small number of the former clergy, and of these, many were occupied in foreign missions. Dreadful as had been the ravages of infidelity and impiety, and the almost entire privation of all spiritual succor, an immense number of the French people still remained faithful to their religion, and a new supply of Levites, to fill the places of those who had perished, was called for on every side. One of the first matters to which the new bishops turned their attention, was the reestablishment of diocesan seminaries, in order to provide for these pressing wants.

These were the circumstances, no doubt, which influenced Bruté to seek admission into the sanctuary. Such a determination could surprise no one who knew him. His whole life, even in the world, had already been a preparation for it. At a different time it would probably have been his first choice—and having chosen it now, he gave himself wholly to the work. He always studied with his pen in hand, and his manuscripts again mark the exactness and extent of his new studies. Theology was a science for which his mind was admirably fitted. He loved his religion, and it evidently became his delight, thoroughly to explore the very foundations of it. In note books made at this time, each subject is developed and illustrated, as if his place had been that of a teacher, instead of a scholar.

Bruté was never a surface student, but now he became emphatically a foundation one. The works of the Fathers of the Church, the acts and canons of her councils, as marking her tradition, were carefully studied by him. From this time until the end of his life, every thing that he read or studied was with this view. His voluminous memoranda show how carefully he recorded everything which might serve to defend, or illustrate the truth, or to expose and confute error. He made the principles of the various sects his careful study, after he came to this country, and could have written a philosophical history of them, if he had seen fit. No one ever made a more faithful and exact use of every moment of his time. He never was idle, and as a consequence of this industry, his tenacious memory enabled him to bring forth from the treasure-house of his mind things new and old.

To assist him in pursuing these studies, he began at this time to collect a library, which became afterwards a large and valuable one, and this may be said to have been the only property he ever owned. Bibliography was also one of his favorite studies, for he understood not only how important a part of knowledge it was to know where learning was to be found, but fully appreciated the value of editions to an accurate student. Although he never wasted a moment over useless books, yet in one sense nothing came amiss to him. He may be said to have been in a good sense of the word a *heluo librorum*.

Bishop Bruté's notes show that he made a retreat in 1806 to ascertain the direction of his vocation. In 1807 his retreat notes show that he was considering work in the foreign missions, with a leaning toward India. He made a plan of going on foot to India. It seems to have afforded him much pleasure to think that his medical studies would prove useful to him in the Asian missions.

It is not necessary to say that to one animated by such dispositions, and so well prepared to make a good use of every opportunity, the four years he spent in the Seminary of St. Sulpice were what the Scripture calls "full years." He advanced alike in solid piety and sound learning. Having completed the usual course, he was, after having passed through the intermediate steps, ordained priest in the Parish Church of St. Sulpice by Monseigneur André, the retired Bishop of Quimper, on the Saturday before Trinity Sunday, 1808.

CHAPTER IX

The Young Priest

THE Bishop of Nantes was very anxious to obtain Father Bruté's services for his diocese, but the Bishop of Rennes, who knew his value not only as an instructor, but as a model for the young Levites of his diocese, appointed him professor of theology in the diocesan seminary. His own spirit of zeal and devotedness seems even at this period to have turned his mind toward the foreign missions. It is evident from the notes of his retreat, that he had already arrived at a great spirit of detachment from home and family (and no one ever loved them more dearly) and was prepared to make all the necessary sacrifices the moment that he felt it to be the will of God that he should leave France. Those who knew him in after times will not be surprised to learn that in the list of sacrifices to be made, if he goes on the foreign missions, that of not being able to carry his library with him occupies a prominent place. At this time (1807) he appears to have determined to go, and I cannot ascertain from his memoranda what induced him to remain. It was probably the authority of the Bishop of Rennes. He had already refused his services to the Bishop of Nantes, and no doubt felt that they were needed at his new seminary. Dr. McCaffrey states that he was also offered the position of assistant chaplain to the Emperor.

In consequence, after his ordination he proceeded to his native city, and entered upon his duties as a professor of theology. The bishop at the same time offered him a canonicate in his cathedral, which dignity he however refused. Although he no doubt discharged with zeal and fidelity his new and important duties, and made use of the opportunity to continue the studies of which he was so fond, yet it is probable he never abandoned his resolution of devoting himself to the missionary life. If he did, a circumstance which happened the following year again renewed it.

The Rev. Benedict Joseph Flaget, of the Society of St. Sulpice, who had already been several years (1792-1808) on the mission in the United States, was nominated in 1808 to the new See of Bardstown in Kentucky. Anxious to escape the proferred dignity, he went to France in the autumn of 1809, in the hope of being permitted to decline it, but on presenting himself to Father Emery, the Superior of St. Sulpice, he found that the Sovereign Pontiff had given an express order that he should accept the office to which he had been called. In consequence, after having remained in France a few months to obtain fellow laborers for his extensive but uncultivated diocese, he returned to the United States in 1810, and was consecrated by Archbishop John Carroll on the 4th of November of that year. It was no doubt his presence in France that renewed in Father Bruté's mind the intention of devoting himself to the foreign missions, and turned his attention towards the United States. Having obtained his bishop's consent, he sailed from Bordeaux in company with Bishop-elect Flaget of Bardstown, in 1810, and arrived in Baltimore on the 10th of August of that year. For nearly two years after his arrival he was assigned as professor of philosophy in the seminary at Baltimore.

Father Bruté always retained the greatest love and veneration for his shipboard companion, Bishop Flaget. He often wrote long letters to him, informing him of news from France, and of mutual friends. His letters also contain many interesting particulars in regard to the history of the Church in this country. One of them was probably his first attempt to write English: "Day of St. Francis of Chantal, Baltimore, being there these two days. Je fuis exilé sur l'Eastern shore of

Maryland, where I serve with Father Monaly, at St. Joseph's, Talbot Co. I went there the first days of vacation. I am trying to learn practically my English. I have said Mass and preached, bad preaching as it may be, in six different places. This must force this dreadful English into my backward head, or I must renounce forever to know it."

After a few months on the mission at St. Joseph's, on the eastern shore of Maryland, he received a letter directing him to go to Mount St. Mary's College, near Emmitsburg, Md., "to aid Father Dubois," as he expresses it. Actually, he was to spend a good part of the remainder of his life there.

CHAPTER X

The Professor on a Mountain

EMMITSBURG would form an admirable subject for a local history, connected with the origin and progress of the Catholic religion in Maryland. The old log chapel at the Elder Station was put up before the Revolution. The village dates back to 1788. The church in the village was built in 1793-4. The Mountain Church was built in 1805-6. The Elder House stood for many years surrounded by virgin forests. It was the place of worship for Catholics for many years. The Elders, Browers, Livres and others were of English descent. It was an influx of Irish Catholics which caused the church in the village to be built. When Mass was first said at Elder Station, the priest came from the lower part of St. Mary's County. The first priest at the village was Father Matthew Ryan.

Father Dubois assembled the people upon the site of the Mountain Church, November 19, 1805. With his usual energy he marked out the spot, and the first tree was felled by him that day. They had a barbecue on the occasion. In 1818, the Sulpicians had the intention of suppressing Mount St. Mary's and selling the property. Father Bruté in one of his notes says: "On 15th June, 1818, Mr. Radford came to see Father Dubois and told him if he was embarrassed in money matters, the inhabitants of Emmitsburg would supply them. Messrs. McNeal, Grover and Boyle offered $1,500."

In 1806 the Sulpicians had established a preparatory

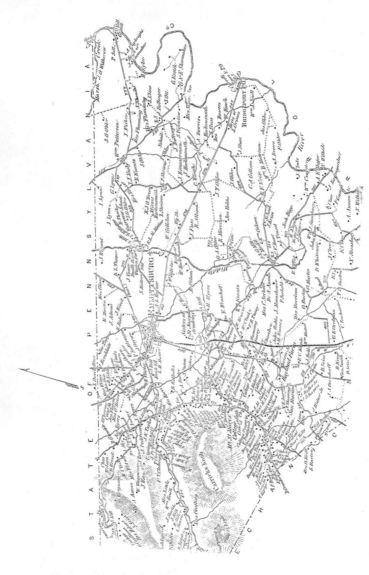

Residents around Emmitsburg at the time of Bishop Bruté

seminary at Pigeon Hill, near Abbotstown, Pa., which was transferred in 1809 to Emmitsburg in Maryland, Father Dubois, who had charge of the mission in that vicinity having already commenced a school there, which afterwards became so well known as Mount St. Mary's College. It was at first intended to be merely a preparatory seminary for ecclesiastical students, but the great advantages it offered for education induced many parents to seek admission for their sons, though not intended for the ecclesiastical state. Father Dubois was president of the college, pastor of Emmitsburg and superior of the new institution of the Sisters of Charity, which had been lately founded at St. Joseph's under the charge of Mother Elizabeth Seton. These varied duties made it necessary that he should have another priest with him. Father Duhamel had relieved him of the charge of the Congregation at Emmitsburg since 1810, but the flourishing condition of the college required additional help, and in consequence Father Bruté was sent to the Mountain for that purpose. This favored spot became from this time, until he was transferred to the bishopric of Vincennes, with the exception of the interval, 1815-18, the theatre of his zeal and holy influence— where all the advantages of his most amiable character, his extensive and profound learning, and eminent Christian and priestly virtues, were exerted with the most beneficial effects.

Father Bruté could never have hoped to have done as much good amongst the inhabitants of India and China, by the exertion of the highest apostolic zeal, as he was permitted to do in this country. It is no disparagement of those holy and eminent men who have adorned the annals of the Catholic Church in America—of a Carroll, a Cheverus, a Dubois and a Flaget—to say that no one has ever exerted a more beneficial influence in favor of the Catholic religion than Bishop Bruté. If Mount St. Mary's, in addition to all the other benefits it has bestowed upon Catholicity in this country, has been in a remarkable degree the nursery of an intelligent, active, zealous priesthood, exactly such as were needed to supply the peculiar wants of the Church in this country, every one, at all acquainted with the history of that institution, will allow that the true ecclesiastical spirit was stamped upon it by Bishop Bruté. His humility, piety and learning made him a model of the Christian priest, and the impression his virtues made upon both ecclesiastical and lay students surpassed all oral instruction. His example confirmed the faith and elevated the character of all who came in contact with him. The name of Bishop Bruté has been, and ever will be, associated with that of Bishop Dubois, as common benefactors to the infant Church in this country.

The Sisters of Charity in this country also owe a debt of gratitude to him. Mother Seton found in him an enlightened director and friend; and his advice and influence was most beneficial to her young community at St. Joseph's. They were both chosen souls upon whom God had bestowed his most precious graces, and strengthened one another like St. Benedict and St. Scholastica by their conferences on spiritual matters. If she revered him as emphatically a man of God, he regarded her as one who, to use his own language, "if placed in circumstances similar to those of St. Theresa, or St. Frances de Chantal, would have been equally remarkable in the scale of sanctity, for it seems to me," he adds, "that there could not be a greater elevation, purity, and love for God, for heaven, and for supernatural and eternal things, than were to be found in her." At her death she left him her Bible, upon the margin of which she had written many notes, which he often quoted and referred to in his classes of theology and Sacred Scripture.

Father Bruté remained at the Mountain, assisting Father Dubois in his various labors in the college, on the mission, and at the sisterhood, until 1815, when he visited France for a short time with the permission of his superior, to bring over his library, and to interest the clergy and people in favor of the missions. He returned in November of the same year, and was appointed president of Saint Mary's College at Baltimore, where he remained until 1818, when on the death of Father Duhamel he again returned to Emmitsburg and resumed his labors, at the College and amongst the Catholics in the vicinity.

THE PROFESSOR ON A MOUNTAIN / 53

Mount St. Mary's College was now thoroughly organized. The students of the theological school connected with it acted as prefects, and assisted as teachers in the institution. This system adopted by Bishop Dubois is liable to some objections; it interferes no doubt with that exact ecclesiastical training, which is justly considered of so much importance. Still even independent of its economical character, it has many advantages, especially for those who are to exercise the holy ministry in a new country, where churches have to be built, and everything formed. The discipline of teaching and governing boys creates habits, most useful under the peculiar difficulties to which a priest is exposed in a country like this. Under such a system, however, it is of the greatest importance that the superior of the seminary should be much more than a mere professor of theology. He should be one fitted to keep before those under his charge the living image of a faithful priest, and capable of forming them to such habits of ecclesiastical virtue as would protect them against the distracting influences of their present duties, as well as the more worldly influences to which they will be exposed in after life. Such a superior in the true sense of the word was Father Bruté. He understood fully all the responsibility which rested upon him, and never did anyone, in his situation, discharge it more faithfully.

A copy of some of his memoranda at this time will give a better idea of his life than any mere generalities.

The following is headed "One day of a Priest, Eternity."

"4½ o'C. *Benedicamus Domino*—'Praise be to God,' on awakening; vocal prayer; meditation before the tabernacle. Rev. Mr. Hickey's Mass; Jesus Christ, my Lord present.

"6 o'C. Celebrated Mass; Jesus Christ present; breakfast; bodily care. Returned to the church (on the Mountain), opened the tabernacle, and took out the Blessed Sacrament. Went with Guy Elder through the woods, our blessed Lord on my breast. Said our beads with acts of devotion to the Blessed Sacrament at the end of each decade.

"8 o'C. At Mrs. McCormick's; her lively marks of faith

and joy; heard her confession; arranged the table; called the people; the young convert and her little one; her husband preparing for his first Communion; administered the Blessed Sacrament to Mrs. McC.; spoke of Martha and Mary and Lazarus and Zaccheus, old friends of our Lord on earth; He still upon earth and we his present living friends. On our way to Emmittsburg, recited the Miserere, our Father, Hail Mary; hymn, 'Jesus lover of my Soul.'

"9½ o'C. At the church in Emmitsburg; opened the tabernacle and ciborium. Went to see Mr.——, 10 years without making his Easter Communion; good *moral* character, as they say; heard his confession; strong faith, gave lively evidences of it; had a talk with him, &c.

"10¾ o'C. Coming back, baptized the child of Peters' wife; her abundant tears; her great difficulties; did not hear her confession at that time.

"11 o'C. Returned to church in Emmitsburg; restored Blessed Sacrament to the ciborium; stopped at Joseph's with Guy; paid a visit to the Blessed Sacrament; saw Mrs. Brawner.

"12 o'C. Found at the college an old German woman waiting for me; no duty for ten years; sick and lame; looked very poorly; came to know if I would hear her; Sister Angela gave her a dinner; to come again on Sunday.

"1½. Was called to see Glacken above Emmitsburg; went to the church of Emmitsburg to get the Blessed Sacrament; this is the fifth time today that I have touched my Sovereign Lord, 'The King of Glory,' as Mr. Duhamel has it, embroidered on the inside door of the tabernacle; carried it to the sick, administered the Sacrament of Extreme Unction; made a little address to those present—several Protestants.

"4 o'C. Went to Mrs. Brawner's; heard her confession; recited my office; Oh! the wonders of that office of the Blessed Sacrament, and am now, writing down these notes; but a thousand details thoughts and acts not told; how wonderful the day of a priest. In the evng. instructions for Confirmation."

On the same paper is written: "What have I done today for the house? Reviewed the 2d Latin class; had a conversation before God, with one of the young men; Latin lesson; reviewed the 3rd French class; Latin lesson to Guy Elder; had a conversation with another young man who came to consult me; one with Mr. Hickey; one with the two Gardiners; wrote a letter; the Dialogue for Baltimore, six pages; spiritual reading, the usual prayers. If all done well what a blessing it would bring; but oh! my Lord, so poorly, by halves —alas!"

On one sheet of paper he has written an account of the manner in which he spent the 3rd Sunday in Advent, at the seminary in Paris, in 1804, when a student there; the 3rd Sunday in Advent at Rennes in 1809, as professor of theology; and the 3rd Sunday in Advent 1819, at the Mountain; the Sundays at Paris and Rennes is the usual exact routine of seminary life in France; the Sunday at Emmitsburg is as follows:

"Slept at the Mountain.

"5 o'C. rose; 1st prayers.

"5½. On my way to the Sisters (at St. Joseph's), meditation 'en route.'

"6 o'C. Heard confessions; wrote out my meditation.

"7 o'C. Mass. Read De Blois' Lives of the Saints.

"8 o'C. Breakfast at Mr. Grover's.

"8¼ o'C. Gave Communion at the church of Emmitsburg to two persons; heard confessions; wrote a meditation.

"10½ o'C. Went to visit Mrs. Hughes and Mrs. Bradley, who are sick; said my 'Little Hours' on the way.

"11½ o'C. Stopped at the Sisters; read the Life of Madame de Chantal; wrote an exhortation for the funeral of Mrs. Lindsay.

"1 o'C. Gave benediction; read the Epistle for the Sunday, and gave a short instruction.

"1½ o'C. Returned to the Mountain. Visited the Sisters at their house [i.e. the Sisters who lived at the Mountain and at that time had charge of the domestic arrangements, infirmary, &c.]; a few words.

"2 o'C. Went to Mr. Elder's; officiated at the Mrs. Lindsay's funeral; exhortation. Read the History of the Councils [i.e. whilst walking, according to custom].

"3 o'C. Vespers; gave benediction; heard confessions after vespers.

"4 o'C. In my room; heard confessions there; office; looked over some Gazettes 1816-17 [French newspapers]; read in the Encyclopedia account of Pennsylvania.

"7 o'C. Supper; study.

"8¾ o'C. Evening prayers; reading, &c."

On another paper, headed "A day of the missions at Emmittsburg"—a holyday at the college, I suppose, he writes down the details of a day's work, spent in going from one family to another, through the country, not visits of friendship or pleasure, but to persons evidently who neglected their duty. He has marked the distances on the margin and they sum up 30 miles. He left the Mountain at 4¾ o'C. in the morning, celebrated Mass at 5½ o'C. at the Sisters at St. Joseph's, and was home at the college, at 6½ in the evening. He sums the day's work by the following memorandum:

"I remember to have spoken to 62 persons, more probably, in regard to matters connected with religion and their duty; made a short exhortation at Mass, it being St. Ignatius's day. Three persons were warned about their Easter duty; several spoken to for circulating evil reports; others warned against attending a camp meeting to begin next week at Hoovers." On another day he writes: "Saturday night, 14th, I received from Baltimore a number of the Edinburg Review, and Stuart against the Eternal Generation of Jesus Christ. Sunday, 15th. Already read through Stuart's book, and wrote a long letter of remarks upon it to Rev. Mr. Elder. Attended to the duties of the day at Emmitsburg. In the evening, read, part on the road, part at home, most of the Edinburg. Monday. This day I finished the Edinburg, made a dozen long notes on the article on O'Meara's Journal, and two on the article upon Duprat's works, with some search amongst my books in regard to points in these memoranda. Wrote a letter to Mr. Chanche; packed up the whole to be sent to Baltimore tomorrow morning by Sister Xavier, who is going there. Finished a map of the Ecclesiastical States for the geography class. Read on the 6th chap. of St. John, Witasse, Tournely, Drouin, Bellarmin, and the Discussion Amicale; consulted also Wesley's Notes, Cajetan, Beil, Bergier, my old notes of Mr. Frayssinous, and noted down twenty-one arguments upon the subject. Taught the class in theology; studied some other questions; taught the class in philosophy; went to a sick call, &c., &c., &c., and then the usual happy round of a priest, prayer, meditation, mass, breviary, beads, visit to the Blessed Sacrament, &c."

The following memorandum was made on the 20th March, 1821: "On the evening of the 14th of March Mr. Damphoux arrived at the Mountain to recall Mr. Hickey to Baltimore, without saying a word to anybody, to speak to the Archbishop and Mr. Tessier, and endeavor to retain him. Stopt at Taneytown at Father Zochi's, and got something to eat. At Winchester found out that I had not a penny in my pocket and was obliged to get my dinner on credit. Arrived at Baltimore (52 miles) 10 minutes before 10 o'C. Mr. Hickey to remain at the college. *Laus Deo.* Set out on my return the next day (16th) in the afternoon; Stopt at Mr. Williamson's, 6½ miles from the city, where the storm obliged me to take refuge. On Saturday, 17th (St. Patrick's day), said Mass, and made a discourse to the people on the text, *'filii sanctorum sumus.'* At 7 o'C. started again, the wind and rain in my face, sometimes so severe, as almost to take away my breath; arrived at the Mountain at 10½ o'C. at night. In going I read 388 pages in D'Anguètil's History of France, the reigns of Louis XII and Francis I; 14 pages of Cicero *de Officiis*; 3 chapters in the New Testament; my office; recited the Chapelet three times. On my journey back, the wind blew so hard, that I could only read a Pamphlet of 25 pages (Documents of the Bishop of Philadelphia) and my office."

During the time that he was thus busily employed in the duties of his station, and training up so many future bishops and priests, he interested himself in anything that could conduce to the refutation of error, and the progress of religion.

He contributed constantly to the Catholic newspapers original articles and often furnished materials for others to use. He carried on a correspondence not only with friends in France, his family and others, but with many distinguished persons in the United States. He assisted Mr. Duponceau in his works on the Indian Languages. He was a friend and correspondent of Charles Carroll of Carrollton, of the distinguished Judge Gaston of North Carolina, and many others.

He took a great interest in the history of the Catholic Church in the United States, and made a large number of notes upon it. During his short episcopate he found time to collect many historical notes in regard to Vincennes and the western country, and wrote several papers for local journals on the subject.

CHAPTER XI

A Man of Influence

WHEN the present Archbishop of Baltimore (Most Rev. F.P. Kenrick) was appointed coadjutor to the aged Bishop of Philadelphia (Dr. Conwell) and Administrator of the Diocese in 1830, and set himself to work to repair the injuries which had been done to Christian piety and Church discipline by that unworthy priest, the Rev. William Hogan and his followers; a task for which his virtues and learning eminently qualified him; Father Bruté interested himself with his usual zeal, in the good works which were undertaken for this purpose, especially the holding of regular diocesan synods and the establishment of a diocesan seminary. The great object of his solicitude always was the formation of an intelligent, zealous clergy, well grounded in the knowledge of theology and Holy Scripture, and able to cope with the peculiar difficulties which stand in the way of Catholics, and the Catholic Religion, in this country.

In furtherance of these views, he warmly approved of Bishop Kenrick's design to prepare a course of theology, adapted to the wants of the Catholic clergy in the United States, where error alike in doctrine and morals presents itself under so many new and startling forms. His numerous letters to Bishop Kenrick upon these subjects not only give evidence of his zeal and piety, and of his high appreciation of the priestly character, but afford specimens of his profound knowledge of theology, and admirable critical skill. He was no mere bookworm, but had great freshness and independence of thought. It might have been supposed that the scenes he had passed through and witnessed in early life would have made him somewhat of an ultra-conservative—one opposed to all change—but it was not so. Though no one could have been more firm than he was in resisting any attempt to alter or modify anything essential to the true character and office of the Church, yet no one understood better the advantages of judicious accommodation to times and circumstances.

When the bishops in the United States began to hold provincial councils, Father Bruté was appealed to from every side, and his advice was constantly asked in regard to those matters which it was their object to arrange. He had from the time of his arrival in this country been anxious that the bishops of the country should assemble in this manner, feeling as he did, how important it was for the progress and stability of religion, not only that they should meet and confer together, but that proper and uniform rules of discipline should be established throughout the country, while it still formed one ecclesiastical province. Many of the beneficial effects which followed the Provincial Councils of Baltimore may be attributed to him.

It was thus, that although apparently hidden in his mountain retreat, engaged in his quiet duties as a professor and missionary, his influence extended on every side, and the whole country may be said in some sense, to have been the field of his labor. No opportunity of doing good escaped his vigilant zeal. If he heard of a rich Catholic who did not make good use of his riches—of one who was lukewarm in the faith—of a priest who was a cause of scandal, or had apostatized—he immediately made use of every influence in his power, to bring them to a sense of their duty. By fervent and touching letters addressed to themselves, and by interesting those who were acquainted with them, he endeavored to infuse into their souls some portion of the spirit of faith and devotion which burned in his own.

His excellent mother died in 1823, and in 1824, he visited his native country to arrange matters connected with her property. His memoranda show, that as usual, every thought of his heart and every moment of his time was occupied with the interest of religion. His visits and conversations were all directed either to the spiritual good of the persons visited, or the benefit of the missions, which he had so much at heart.

He took advantage of this visit to make a long retreat at the Solitude of Iffy. I have in my possession the notes of this and of all his retreats. They contain abundant evidence of his progress in solid piety and the most intimate union with God. He returned to America in autumn, and resumed his duties at Mount St. Mary's.

In 1832, when the cholera had commenced its ravages with so much violence in Canada, and its immediate extension to the United States was anticipated, he wrote to the Archbishop of Baltimore (Whitfield) offering his services, when it should reach that city. In August, Father Deluol visited Mount St. Mary's, and the pestilence having broken out in Baltimore, Father Bruté returned with him in order to attend upon the sick. Immediately after his arrival, he had a violent attack of intermittent fever, and was obliged to return to the Mountain; but as soon as he had recovered, he set off again, without saying a word to anyone, for Baltimore, and labored in the cholera hospitals there, until his services were no longer needed.

One of the subjects, as connected with the progress and solid establishment of religion in this country which constantly occupied Father Bruté's thoughts, and upon which he often dwelt in his letters to Bishop Flaget and others, was the necessity of multiplying episcopal sees as fast as they were needed, and fit subjects could be found to fill them. He was destined, in the order of God's providence, to cooperate in the work, not only by his advice and exhortations, but by his active exertions. The Fathers of the 2d Provincial Council of Baltimore in 1833, requested the Sovereign Pontiff (Gregory XVI) to erect the town of Vincennes in Indiana, into a bishopric, having jurisdiction over the State of Indiana and a part of Illinois, and Father Bruté was, on their recommendation, appointed to be its first bishop. When the news reached him, his humility, and strong sense of accountability, caused him at first to shrink from the burden which was about to be placed upon his shoulders. With all his zeal and activity, he was very diffident of his fitness for the office, and in one of his written examinations, in which according to his usual custom he states with great simplicity the two sides of the case, he makes out, according to his own view of the matter, a very formidable list of defects; but when he found that the matter was settled, he went to work, not only with the zeal of a good priest, but the vivacity and energy of a true Frenchman. His only real defect was his imperfect English pronunciation. He may be said to have had every other qualification—natural talent—industrious and methodical habits—great erudition—a high sense of duty—a great spirit of self-sacrifice and all directed by a will and energy of character which nothing could dishearten or overcome. I have been told that when the matter of his nomination to the new see was debated in the council, Bishop England was opposed to it, thinking that on account of his love of books and study, he would not be fitted for the office of a missionary bishop in the backwoods; but with Bishop Bruté, *duty* was the first point, and Bishop England and everyone else who witnessed his short career as a bishop, must have been surprised at the energy and self-devotion which he manifested. In administrative talent in particular, a great point in a new country, where everything has to be created as it were, he surprised those who knew him best.

At the time he received the Papal Bulls announcing his appointment as Bishop of Vincennes (May, 1834), he was giving a retreat to the Sisters at St. Joseph's. He opened the documents in the chapel on his knees. The next day he went to Baltimore and made a retreat in the seminary, to decide whether to accept or refuse. Every possible consideration on either side was drawn out with the acuteness of a practiced lawyer.

As soon as he had accepted the Bulls, he made the necessary arrangements for his consecration, and prepared to set out for the new and arduous field of labors, to which the few remaining years of his life were to be devoted. It is evident from his letters, that he tore himself away from Mount St. Mary's with the greatest reluctance. It had bound itself around his warm French heart as a second home.

CHAPTER XII

Bishop on Horseback

I FIND among his manuscripts notes of a letter apparently
written to the Leopoldine Association of Vienna, in return
for some assistance it had given him, and which relates
many interesting circumstances connected with his taking
possession of his diocese, and his first labors there. Whether
it has ever been published, I do not know: "Mere words,"
he writes, "will poorly express the gratitude of the Bishop
of Vincennes for the offering of love and zeal, which your
benevolent association has been pleased, in the name of God,
to bestow upon his newly created diocese. The merits of the
gift, are secure for heaven, for the pious benefactors—may I
have my share in them, by making a faithful use of what has
been thus committed to my stewardship. It is perhaps proper,
that in return, I should give you some information in regard
to the beginnings of the diocese, which has been the object
of your bounty.

"When I arrived in Baltimore from France in 1810, to
devote myself to the missions in this country, there was but
one bishop for the whole United States, the late Most Rev.
John Carroll. Since then many other sees have been erected—the See of Detroit erected in 1833, was the twelfth. The
See of Vincennes, erected in 1834, by the Holy See, at the
recommendation of the 2d Provincial Council of Baltimore,
may be regarded as the 13th. To this see, thus established,

65

Map drawn by Bishop Bruté

I was named as the first bishop. At the time of my appointment I was and had been for many years, superior and professor of theology in the seminary, connected with the College of Mount St. Mary's, near Emmitsburg, in Maryland. Although a large number of priests now on the mission in the United States had been sent out from this seminary, at the time of my appointment, they were not able to aid me, either with priests or money. The Sisters of Charity at St. Joseph's, the Mother House, made me a present of two hundred dollars to assist me in establishing myself at Vincennes. On my way to Bardstown, where I was to make my retreat previous to my consecration, I visited my respected friend Dr. Purcell, the Bishop of Cincinnati, whose diocese must always continue to be a most worthy object of your generosity, as having a large population of German Catholics. He kindly accompanied me as far as Louisville and then returned, whilst I proceeded on my way to Bardstown, where I once more had the happiness of meeting, my father and friend, the venerable Bishop Flaget, the Patriarch of these western missions, upon which he has laboured above 43 years—twenty-five of which as Bishop of Bardstown, having jurisdiction over the whole western country. I was also permitted once more to embrace my old friend Bishop David, who having resigned the Coadjutorship of Bardstown, has been succeeded by Bishop Chabrat.

"At the time of my arrival Bishop Flaget was about leaving for Cincinnati, to consecrate the large German Church which had been lately erected. I spent a few days in visiting the different institutions of the diocese, the college and seminary at Bardstown, the beautiful institution of the Sisters of Charity of Nazareth, founded by Bishop David, the House of the Sisters of Loretto, founded by the Rev. Mr. Nerinckx, both having several academies and schools under their care. I visited also the flourishing College of the Jesuits (St. Mary's), and regretted very much that my time would not allow of my going to the Dominican Convent and Novitiate of St. Rose. By the time I had finished my retreat (from 4th to 12th Oct.) under Bishop David, Bishop Flaget had returned from Cincinnati and I set out with him for Louisville where Bishop Purcell joined us. Crossing the Ohio, we proceeded directly towards St. Louis, across the vast prairies of Illinois, and passing through the town of Vincennes, half incognito. It was a source of great happiness and consolation to me, to pass so many days in the company of these holy bishops, and to meet that most excellent prelate, Dr. Rosati of St. Louis. On the 26th of October, assisted by Bishops Flaget and Purcell, he consecrated his new and beautiful cathedral, which was an occasion of great joy to the whole city. A large body of the militia, and even the United States Troops, from the barracks near St. Louis, assisted at the ceremony. Two days after, on the 28th of October, the day of the Holy Apostles, St. Simon (my patron) and St. Jude, I was consecrated in the same cathedral, by the Rt. Rev. Bishop Flaget, assisted by Bishop Rosati and Bishop Purcell. The sermon for the occasion was preached by the Rev. Mr. Hitzelberger. On the Festival of all Saints, at the request of Bishop Rosati I officiated pontifically, for the first time. During these days, which was a time of general festivity, there were sermons, each morning and evening, preached by the bishops, or some of the Jesuit Fathers, who have a large and flourishing college at this place, at present our farthest western point, a thousand miles distant from New York, but with another thousand miles of territory extending beyond it to the Pacific, the only frontier of these vast United States.

"Having left St. Louis, with Bishops Flaget, and Purcell, the Rev. Messrs. Abel and Hitzelberger and Father Petit, we arrived at Vincennes the 5th of November. Some miles before reaching the city, we were met by a number of the citizens, Catholics and Protestants, on horseback, who had accompanied the pastor, the Rev. Mr. Lalumière, a native of the state, and the first priest ordained (by Bishop Flaget) for Vincennes. He was of course filled with joy, in seeing a bishop granted to his Indiana, and all the inhabitants seemed to share in it.

"The ceremony of the installation took place the same

evening. Bishop Flaget, who 43 years before had been the missionary priest here, when it was a simple trading and military post, in the midst of the surrounding wilderness, proceeded to address the people with his usual fervor. Venerated and loved by all, himself in the 74th year of his age, he introduced to them their new bishop, no longer young, being in his 54th year, and urged them to make a good use of the privileges which God in his mercy had bestowed upon them. Other instructions were given during these days. On Sunday, I officiated pontifically, and on Monday my venerable colleagues took their leave, amidst the blessing of the whole population, to return to their respective dioceses. They literally left me alone. Father Petit was obliged soon to return to his college in Kentucky. Mr. Lalumière took charge of the missions in the vicinity of Vincennes, but still 25 or 30 miles distant, and in the whole diocese, there were but two other priests, one, Mr. Ferneding, in charge of the German missions 150 miles distant, and Mr. St. Cyr, whom Bishop Rosati had permitted to assist me for one year, and who was stationed at Chicago, 225 miles off.

"The Cathedral Church, a plain brick building 115 feet long and 60 broad, consisting of the four walls and roof, unplastered and not even whitewashed—no sanctuary—not even a place for preserving the vestments and sacred vessels. Only a simple altar of wood with a neatly gilded tabernacle, and a cross and six beautiful candlesticks, a gift from France, which were much in contrast with the poverty and utter destitution of the place. The house built for the missionary, and now the episcopal residence, consists of a small, comfortable room and closet, 25 feet by 12, without however a cellar under, or a garret above; a small plot for a garden lays between it and the church, on the other side of which is the Catholic cemetery. Some years since, the town had a common burying ground prepared, beyond its limits, and insisted for a while that the Catholics should bury their dead in it like the rest; but they resisted so resolutely they were at last permitted to bury in their own cemetery. An old wooden building a short distance from the *Palace,* is occupied by the servant, and near it is a stable ready for the bishop's horse, when he is able to get one. The people are mostly of French descent, poor, illiterate, but of that open, lively disposition, which bespeaks their origin. They retain their faith—love their priest, but are negligent in attending to their religious duties. They are very remiss also in teaching their children their prayers, and the catechism, and this causes them to forget it themselves. Many also are in the habit of using profane language. It is true and should be mentioned, that of late years they have been much neglected, and much of their former piety seems now to be rekindling in their hearts.

"The kind reception I met with on my arrival, was followed up by generous gifts of provisions and other necessary things. Of money they have little, and consequently can give but little. A subscription list which was handed around some months after I came, with the intention of providing a yearly income for my support did not reach two hundred dollars, and most of this was to be paid in grain, if they had not the money at the time. It may seem somewhat out of place for me to enter into such details, but they are necessary to show that although a parish priest, accustomed to the simplicity of seminary life, may find a sufficient support, yet the resources of the diocese are entirely inadequate to provide for its great and urgent wants, the education of young men intended for the priesthood, and building up of those institutions of charity for orphans and others, without which religion can never be firmly established. The revenue from pews in my cathedral is so small as barely to supply what is necessary for the altar and current expenses of the church itself. Of some property which belongs to the diocese, but which at present brings no income, I will have occasion to speak hereafter.

"As the directors of your association very properly request minute details, in order to be able to form an accurate opinion, I will proceed to give an account of the first six or eight months of my administration.

"A few days after the bishops who so kindly accompa-

nied me to Vincennes had left, I went with the Rev. M. Lalumière to visit his two missions, or congregations as they
are generally named in this country—first to St. Peter's and
then to St. Mary's. The last was not quite completed, and
I was requested to name it. It was a great happiness to me
to put the first church, which I was called upon to bless in
my new diocese under the patronage of the blessed mother of
God; so I named it St. Mary's, and promised to return again
in two weeks and bless it, when it was finished. On the
day appointed, all the good people assembled with their
worthy pastor M. Lalumière at the little chapel. It was built
of logs, as almost all the buildings still are in this part of
the country. It is only about from 15 to 20 years since these
settlements were made. There are about 150 Catholic families, most of them from Kentucky, but some from Ireland.
We formed a procession and went around the chapel and the
ceremonies were observed as closely as possible; then I celebrated Mass and gave an instruction to those who were
present. Some baptisms and a marriage filled up the labors
of the day, marked as the first, on which I blessed a church
in the wilderness. The conduct of the people was full of edi-
fication.

"Afterwards I visited some of the places around Vincennes where I found small clusters of Catholic families. At
the Cat's river, 13 miles from the town, I had more than
25 or 30 families to attend, and every time I went there I
saw how much more good would be done by a resident
pastor. I will soon send one to them, though for the first
few years he will have to be supported chiefly from the
means at the bishop's disposal. Once they are firmly rooted
however such missions will support themselves. The people
are mostly of French origin. I visited another congregation
in Edgar County on the Illinois side of the diocese, about 70
miles from Vincennes. It is an American settlement from
Kentucky with some Irish families among them. There are
perhaps 50 or 60 families within a circuit of 15 miles, and
I found them as at St. Mary's truly zealous for their religion, and talking of the church which they would soon

build, and of the priest that would soon be sent to them.

"At Vincennes I undertook to bring our long neglected youths to their first Communion. At Christmas I had twenty, some of whom I had prepared myself as well as I could. Others I put off, intending to prepare them during the Lent. Sixty more made their first Communion at Easter, many of them 17, 18 and 20 years old. The following Sunday I administered the Sacrament of Confirmation for the first time in the Cathedral of St. Francis Xavier to about 90, mostly the same who had just made their first Communion. I say nothing of the difficulty of the task as it would look as if I were commending exertions, the poor results of which I have rather to lament before God. I simply mention what may give the association a proper idea of the task of the bishop, and of the situation of the newly erected diocese.

"Having a population of about 1500 souls under my immediate pastoral care, every Sunday I had to give two instructions, one in French, and one in English, and then to administer the sacraments. In the eight months I had 65 baptisms, 10 marriages, and 20 burials, and a great many sick calls to attend, often six, seven and ten miles from home. Then there were a number of other visits to be made, poor to be seen to, Protestants to instruct, etc. I received four men into the Church, two of them upon their death bed.

"Much of my time was also taken up by the extensive correspondence which devolved upon me as soon as I was sent to Vincennes, and also by the numerous communications I continued writing, as I had long been in the habit of doing, for the religious papers, particularly the Catholic Telegraph of Cincinnati. That kind of work is continually called for by our position in this country, and the influence exerted by it too important to allow it to be neglected. Over the signature of 'Vincennes' a series of letters were published in which the ancient labors of the Society of Jesus in this region, from the Lakes to the Mississippi, were described. Our very town took its name from a French officer, M. de Vincennes, who was massacred an age ago by the

Indians, together with a Jesuit Father who had accompanied him in an expedition to protect the friendly tribes who lived upon the Wabash, where the Society had established the mission of St. Francis Xavier. Others of these communications consisted of a sketch of the country and its aborigines, an account of the former difficulties which religion had had to contend with, her obscure and precarious beginning, her present hopes, the inducements offered now to Catholic settlers, and also the steps taken by the last council to obtain the erection of the new diocese, comprising Indiana and a part of Illinois. They were followed by an account of our present transactions, and a pastoral letter which I had given after my consecration and which had been published in the newspapers of Vincennes, and in all our Catholic journals. In that letter the Protestants themselves were affectionately addressed, and the intentions of the American Bishops and our Holy Father at Rome were explained in such a plain and simple way that left no room for the absurd charge of their being influenced by political, and not simply religious considerations, and that no foreign conspiracy or danger, for the civil institutions of America were involved in this new carrying out of the original divine commission given to the Church by her Lord: 'Go and teach all nations.'

"Being convinced of the fact that we could not obtain missionaries from the other dioceses, I determined to try to obtain some from abroad. Before setting out however for this purpose, I wished to examine myself the west and north of the diocese while M. Lalumière would go through the south and east and make a report of his observations to me, so that I could start without much delay on the journey in which I am now engaged. After Easter in company with an honest and pious man of Vincennes I went through Illinois, visiting again Edgar county for the paschal duty, and then proceeding north as far as Chicago on Lake Michigan. Mr. S. Cyr had arrived there from St. Louis and enabled the Catholics to make their Easter Communions, so I gave only a few confirmations, and three instructions, one on Saturday and two on Sunday to encourage the rising Catholic congregation of that most important point. It is now composed of about 400 souls of all countries, French, Canadians, Americans, Irish, and a good number of Germans. The garrison of the fort, the commandant, and part of the staff and band of musicians attended. In general it may be said that the military are always friendly to the Catholics and their services, which they are free to attend if they choose.

"From Chicago we went round the end of Lake Michigan to the River St. Joseph and the mission of the Rev. Mr. De Seille at the Indian Village of Pokegan, situated just outside our diocese, and in that of Detroit. This mission was established many years ago by the venerable Mr. Badin. Mr. De Seille has lived for three or four years at Pokegan's Village. He has there and in the neighborhood more than 650 Catholic Indians baptized. A large number of their huts are built around the chapel, which is constructed of bark with a cross erected behind and rising above it, and filled with rudely made benches. The Indians begin and end their work without hammer, saw or nails; the axe being their only implement, and bits of skin or bark serving to fasten the pieces together. The room of the missionary is over the chapel, the floor of the one forming the ceiling of the other. A ladder in the corner leads to it, and his furniture consists, as did the prophet's, of a table and chair, and a bed, or rather a hammock swung on ropes. Around the room are his books, and the trunks which contain the articles used in the chapel, as well as his own apparel. He spends his life with his good people sharing their corn and meat, with water for his drink, and tea made from the herbs of his little garden. He abjures all spirits, as all the Catholic Indians are forbidden to touch that which is the bane of their race, and he would encourage them by his example. I attended at the evening catechism, prayers and canticles, and in the morning said Mass, at which a large number assisted. Through the interpreter I addressed a few words to them.

"On Thursday evening we arrived at South Bend, a little town beautifully situated on the high banks of the St.

Joseph River. It is growing rapidly owing to its many advantages. Crossing the river we visited 'St. Mary of the Lake,' the mission house of the excellent Mr. Badin who has lately removed to Cincinnati. He had a school there kept by two sisters who have also gone away, leaving the place vacant. The 625 acres of land attached to it, and the small lake named St. Mary's, make it a most desirable spot, and one day soon I hope to be occupied by some prosperous institution. Rev. Mr. Badin has transferred it to the bishop on the condition of his assuming the debts, a trifling consideration compared with the importance of the place.

"On Friday morning we left for the Tippecanoe river and the village of Chickakos. The Indians had heard of our coming, and had sent some of their number in advance to ascertain our movements. They gave notice of our approach to others who had camped out a few miles to wait for the bishop, and make a more worthy escort for him. The Chief Chickakos was there and directed their movements. Coffee had been prepared at a small village only three miles from the principal one. We dismounted, and sitting on mats of woven straw partook of their kind cheer. Then we crossed the river, and soon arrived. On our way Mr. De Seille pointed to a poor mother sitting on the bank with an infant child lying in her lap who had been recently baptized and was now near death. He told me that it would be a great consolation to her if I would give her my blessing, and tell her her of the happiness awaiting her little angel. I did so, and could see by her silent and resigned expression that she felt comforted.

"Chickakos Village is not so large as Pokegan, yet the chapel is nearly as large. It is however, without ceiling, and without a room for the missionary overhead. The mission being of later standing, Mr. De Seille had baptized only about 120 persons, of whom I confirmed 16. He was to remain there two weeks to prepare many more for baptism and some for their first Communion. He said he found some difficulty in preparing the Indians for their first Communion on account of his not being sufficiently master of their language to make use of the proper terms in treating of the Holy Eucharist. He begins to understand it now, yet when he speaks to them he prefers to do so through his interpreter, a Canadian woman born of an Indian mother, a truly excellent and deserving person. She is 70 years of age and yet preserves a strength and activity truly wonderful. She followed us on horseback, and was very ready to assist us.

"On our arrival all assembled at the chapel, and Mr. de Seille introduced me to them as their bishop, the head in these parts of all the other 'Robes Noires' (Black Robes), the name which they have given to the Catholic priests, or Jesuits, for it is all one to them. He added that I had no one above me, on earth, but the great 'Robe Noire' beyond the high seas, the Chief of all the Christians, in the world, meaning the Pope. He said that every 'Robe Noire' that would come to them must come as sent by the bishop, and then be received; otherwise they should have nothing to do with them. The Chief Chickakos said a few words in reply to show that they were well pleased, and promising that they would meet together the next morning to give a more special expression to their feelings.

"Accordingly on the Sunday morning, having informed us that they were ready, Mr. De Seille and myself sat upon two little stools in the chapel, and some twelve of the leading men came in and took their seats upon some of the opposite benches. Chickakos made the speech, and I was very much struck with the concluding sentence of it, when, raising his eyes and his arm towards heaven, and then pointing to the ground, having previously expressed their confidence in Father de Seille, and in me, and their readiness to receive me as their bishop, and their desire to show it by presenting me with half a section, 320 acres, of their land, he said that 'God, when He would return from heaven to visit our earth would see that ground, to which he pointed, which they were giving me, and that it would prove to Him their sincere devotion to His holy religion and the messengers he had sent to secure its blessings to them.' To this I replied through the good interpreter.

"We then made our preparations for Mass, and the administration of the Sacrament of Confirmation. Before Mass
six children were baptized by me. My instruction was on
prayer, and the gifts of the Holy Ghost. Mr. de Seille told me
that he had observed in them all such a deep sense of
the eminent privilege of prayer, and the dispositions it required, such as are not found, as often as they should be,
among the best instructed Christians of more favored countries. I saw most unequivocal evidence of it in their be-
havior in the chapel, and the affecting, earnest way in which
they listened to the instructions, repeated their prayers, and
sang their hymns, and I was very much edified. Of the
16 that I confirmed, one was an old Chief who since his
baptism had led such an innocent life, that he had not been
observed to commit any fault, or give way to impatience, or
any other imperfection.

"We slept on the benches of the chapel, and some of
the straw from the floor, wrapped up in our great coats after
the manner of the good father. Our food was boiled corn,
fish, venison, and wild turkey, minced together in one dish,
and some cranberries broken and mixed with sugar they get
from trees. Our drink was water. Coffee was not to be had
although this was the principal village.

"In the afternoon vespers were sung in Ottawa, and
as I should have mentioned before, by the aid of printed
books. Many used them, as they are very quick in learning
to read, and have retentive memories. Some knew the whole
contents of their prayer books. They contain all the usual
daily prayers, and exercises for Confession and Communion, a pretty long catechism, and a large number of canticles, with many of the principal hymns and anthems of the
Church. Among others they have the 'Pange Lingua' and
the Psalms for Vespers translated in Ottawa.

"I was to leave them after vespers, so before we began,
they came to sign the deed of the land presented to the
Church, which we had drawn up in as legal a form as we
could, putting the indispensable condition that the act was
subject to the approval of their temporal Father at Wash-

ington, as they call the President of the United States. Although many know how to read, none know how to write, so Chickakos and some of his friends made their marks on the paper, and two Canadian traders who were present, signed their names as witnesses. It remains now to be ratified by the President.

"After a few parting words, and giving them my blessing, we mounted our horses, and were escorted for some miles by a large number, Chickakos at their head, who before leaving us, dismounted from their horses, and asked their bishop's blessing again. Mr. De Seille was to remain two weeks there giving instructions, and preparing the Indians for Baptism and first Communion. Some time after I received in Vincennes two long letters from that excellent missionary, giving me a most interesting account of the exercises of the two weeks which he had spent there, at the end of which he had baptized 80, and admitted 30 to their first Communion. He said that the coming of a bishop, 'a chief man of the true prayer,' as they called him, and head of the 'Robes Noires,' had excited much joy among all the Indians. They remembered when the Jesuits left the country, after the conquest of Canada by the English, how their fathers had hoped until their death for their return, and dying without that consolation most earnestly recommended to their children to be looking for them when they should come, and to receive them and believe them to be the true messengers of God.

"We spent the night at the house of a settler 15 miles from Chickakos, and found the house so full that many had to lie on the floor, as I had done once on my way to the lake. Here we had a bed for two, as was often the case. Through all that journey of 600 miles we seldom came to any regular taverns, but almost every family would allow you to share their meals, and give you a place under their roof, receiving on your departure a small compensation, which however is sufficient to remunerate them. Our old friend, for one's evening's acquaintance establishes that relation between us, told me in the morning, when I asked for the bill, that he used to take nothing, but as he could not well stand that, and wished still to help any stranger, he only took what strictly sufficed. He was of the sect called 'Christians.' After supper he had said to us, 'Friends, I ought not to interrupt our family rule on your account; we are about to have our evening devotions. You can remain with us, or if you prefer to retire I will show you your room.' We thanked him, and said that we would rather retire. This did not displease him at all, or prevent him from bestowing every attention upon us. We were almost always treated kindly by all.

"I improved in every family such opportunities of conversation as were afforded me, and passed such simple remarks as would make them acquainted with our faith and practices, and remove some of the prejudices which they had acquired from their parents or the ministers of the places, from which they had come to settle in the West. They listened to what I had to say, and as very few ministers have as yet come to these remote parts, I found that it would be easy to preoccupy the ground. But alas we have not the means to do so, nor priests enough to send to the dispersed sheep of the house of Israel, to the domestics of the faith exposed to lose it almost as easily as these Protestants are to acquire it.

"The day after we reached Logansport, a rapidly improving town on the canal that is nearly completed, and will unite the Wabash with the Maumee at Fort Wayne, and thus Lake Erie with the Ohio, and the Mississippi through the States of Indiana and Illinois. I found there a good number of Catholics and promised to send them one of the first priests I could obtain. I said Mass the next morning and then left for home, yet some days' journey, passing through Fayetteville, Attica, Covington, Terre Haute, etc. Few Catholics are as yet collected in these growing towns, but soon there will be more. Had I said Mass at Terre Haute about 20 Catholics might have been present, and many Protestants joining them, and in our new country that is a sufficient indication to send a missionary.

"By this very visit to Europe I trust to obtain some

whom I will be able to support with the generous gift of the association, and thus place Terre Haute, and many other such towns on the line of missionary round. I have myself heard in the city of Baltimore the interesting account of those who remembered to have had Mass said in their room by a missionary, there being no resident pastor; Baltimore, where now five parish churches, one splendid cathedral, one seminary, and five private chapels in the different communities and hospitals, make twelve sanctuaries in which the 21 priests living with their archbishop in that metropolis, officiate. Poor Diocese of Vincennes! Let us however put trust in God, and what a change can a few years, through His blessing and the perseverance of zealous souls, effect.

"Shortly after my return, Mr. Lalumière came home, and the account of his journey was very consoling. He had found more Catholics than I had, and many places ready to receive a priest. In three places they had begun to build churches. At Fort Wayne they were finishing one, 60 feet by 30, and the congregation numbers 150 Catholic families. I was happy to send to them the Rev. M. Ruff from Metz in France, recently ordained, and speaking the three languages used there, French, English and German. Of the latter there are a good many living there and in the environs. I had ordained Mr. Ruff, subdeacon and deacon, before my journey to Chicago, and had sent him to the Seminary of St. Louis (St. Mary of the Barrens) to make his retreat, and there he was ordained priest by that excellent prelate, Dr. Rosati.

"We have as yet no seminary, no college, no religious establishment in any part of the diocese, except an academy and school kept in Vincennes by four Sisters of Charity from the House of Nazareth in Kentucky. They had been recalled to Nazareth some months before I came. My first care was to secure their return, and they resumed their school the end of April. When I left they had four boarders and about fifty day scholars."

As soon as he arrived at his diocese, he perceived immediately, that in order to provide for its urgent wants, it would be necessary to obtain priests from Europe—the harvest was already ripe, or rather was perishing for want of some one to gather it in, and it would not do to wait until they had found or raised up laborers from among themselves. He determined however to make the above described visitation in order to understand the extent, and exact nature of its necessities, from personal observation. In his letters to his friends, describing his journey, he enters into many details, which are omitted in his communication to the Leopoldine Association, as not becoming the gravity of what may be regarded as an official document.

In one letter he speaks of having traveled 550 miles on horseback in the last six weeks. He describes very graphically the little groups of emigrants whom he fell in with, exploring the country and seeking new homes—his conversations with them, and the scattered residents, taking advantage of every opportunity, in a quiet, unobtrusive manner, to do away with their prejudices in regard to the Catholic Church, and to instruct them in its real doctrines and principles. Whenever he heard of a Catholic family, he spared no labor or fatigue to find them and visit them. His descriptions of their lonely situation in the then wilderness are very touching. Sometimes it is a poor Negro with his family, emigrants from Maryland or Kentucky, living in the woods, all crowding to the door to welcome the bishop and get his blessing. Sometimes a respectable white family, brought up amid Catholic privileges, now without priest or Mass, or Catholic neighbors, and often exhibiting the sad effect of such privations.

Cathedral of St. Francis Xavier, 1834, as sketched by Bishop Bruté

CHAPTER XIII

'Good Bishop Bruté'

BUT in all of Bishop Bruté's letters there is not a word of murmuring, or an expression of discouragement. His whole life had been an act of conscientious and ever increasing self-devotion—and the difficulties which now stood in his way only served to increase his zeal and activity. As soon as he had made himself acquainted with the condition of his diocese, he immediately took the necessary steps to provide for its wants so far as was in his power. His heart instinctively turned to his own country in the hour of need, and he again crossed the ocean to seek for missionaries and for such pecuniary help as would enable him to finish his cathedral and provide schools for education of the young. His notes and memoranda indicate that he found himself very much out of place in the courts and among the grand personages, with whom his office and the object of his journey brought him in contact. He was received however everywhere with the greatest kindness. He took advantage of the opportunity to visit the chair of the Apostle and to receive for himself and his diocese the benediction of the common Father of the Faithful, and then hastened back to his home in the wilderness.

A warm welcome awaited him, on his return to his episcopal city, for all alike, Protestants as well as Catholics, had become very much attached to their good bishop. And now commenced a new series of labors which were to end only with his life, which was drawing to its close. With the resources which had been placed at his disposal in Europe, he established a diocesan college seminary in his episcopal city—an orphan asylum and a free school. The surplus was spent in finishing his cathedral and in helping to erect small churches at certain points where they were most needed.

He brought twenty priests and seminarians with him from France, but though his health had already begun to fail, he still performed the work of one in the vigor and freshness of early manhood. He had caught a fever, while riding on the outside of a stage coach in Ohio, on his way to the Council of Baltimore in 1837, which ended in consumption. Bishop Bruté was tall in stature and thin, but naturally very strong and vigorous. He never took recreation in the ordinary sense of the word. His features were plain, but his face was full of intelligence, and marked by that peculiar sweetness of expression, which has often been noted in the countenances of very holy persons—a radiance which came from the pure and holy soul within, and which often made a vivid impression upon those who approached him. He never would permit a likeness to be taken, and the only portrait of him which exists was from a cast, taken after his death. It gives a very good representation of his features.

At home, he was at once the bishop, the pastor of the congregation, the professor of theology for his seminary, and a teacher for one of his academies. He wrote twice a month to every priest in his diocese, and thus communicated to them a portion of that zeal for the glory of God, and the salvation of souls, which formed the constant object of his every thought and action. He visited every portion of his diocese repeatedly, and wherever he went, he engaged in all the duties of an ordinary pastor. Indiana and Illinois had at this time, as is well known, embarked largely in that immense system of internal improvements, which for the time being, ended so disastrously. The laborers upon them, mostly Irish emigrants, suffered greatly from the cholera and malignant fevers.

One of the great afflictions which Bishop Bruté had to

suffer, was being unable to provide for the spiritual wants of these poor people, whose lively faith and generous impulsive nature, had attached him very warmly to them. He often went among them himself—heard their confessions—celebrated Mass for them in their miserable cabins, and prepared the sick and dying for the awful passage to eternity.

In the words of Dr. McCaffrey, "Difficulties that would have disheartened almost any one else, only served to increase his zeal and charity. Having commenced a journey of four hundred miles in such a state of bodily suffering that he could not sit upright on his horse, he nevertheless completed it without the intermission of a single day. Shortly before his death, he left Vincennes to visit a distant mission, which he had already visited thrice within the year, and though so weak and extenuated, that he could scarcely support his tottering frame, in the absence of the pastor, he attended to three distant sick-calls, on the same day, and almost dying, administered the consolations of religion to those, who appeared no nearer mortal dissolution than himself."

It was the same with him until the last moment. His resolute will and fervent zeal seemed to triumph over painful and debilitating disease which was destroying his body; and when no longer able to work himself, he cheered on those who were engaged in the task, with words full of courage and enthusiasm. His letters at this period also bring still more strongly in relief, on account of his inability to labor himself, a point in his character, for which he had always been remarkable, his kind consideration for others. It seemed to grieve him to give orders, without being able to take his share of the labor necessary to carry them into execution. Among the priests of his diocese at this time was the Rev. Michael Shaw, a convert to the Catholic Church, who had formerly, I believe, been an officer in the British army. Father Shaw erected the first church at Madison, Indiana. The difficulties he encountered were very great. The bishop was much attracted to this good priest and did all he could to aid and encourage him. I have in my possession a large number of notes and letters which the good bishop wrote to him, during the last years of his life. They are entirely unstudied—written upon the spur of the moment, but are full of interest, not only as exhibiting all the beautiful traits of his character —his lively faith—his active usefulness, and his ardent zeal —but also as giving an insight into the nature of his administration. It was characterized as I have remarked, by the most untiring energy and perseverance. No good work once undertaken, was ever allowed to stand still; and it is impossible to understand how so much was done in so short a time, especially as most of it was accomplished while the States of Illinois and Indiana were laboring under the most severe financial embarrassments.

The Bishop had a great horror of running into debt. Personally, he cared nothing about money. Father Hickey said, "If he had five dollars in his pocket, it went to the first person who asked for it. His clothing was very plain, and he often gave away everything except what he had on his back; and even these were not safe, for he was known to give away these to poor Negroes he was accustomed to visit."

But at length the poor body, to which he had given little rest for so many years, refused to do its work any longer. I cannot better describe the closing scenes of his eventful, and well spent life, than in the words of the beautiful discourse by Father McCaffrey from which I have so often quoted. Its author received the details from the mouths of those who had witnessed them.

"Death," he says, "which could be no unwelcome visitor to one whose thoughts, hopes and affections all centered in a better world, found him full-handed of good works, and longing only to be dissolved and to be with Christ. Invincibly patient and resigned under the severest suffering, full of tender piety, calm, collected and brightly exhibiting his characteristic virtues to the last, he set a beautiful example of the manner in which a Christian should prepare himself to run his final race and to win the crown of a glorious immortality. As his strength diminished, his devotion increased. He sought no alleviation for his sufferings: on the contrary he was eager still to labor and endure, in the two fold view of doing good to others and resembling more his crucified Savior. When unable to walk or stand, he would at least sit up, and write to any whom he could hope to benefit by his correspondence; and to those around him he would speak on pious subjects, such as the love of God, conformity to His holy will, or devotion to the Blessed Virgin, with the unction of a saint, and the ardour of a seraph. But six hours before his death, he wrote with his own hand, and not without much difficulty and pain, several moving letters to persons, who had unfortunately abandoned the practice of their faith, and to whom he wished to make this dying appeal in behalf of their souls, while the portals of eternity were closing upon him.

"These last precious days of his life were thus entirely taken up in the works of charity, in instructing, edifying and consoling those who were with him, and in intimate and affectionate communion with his God, whom he hoped soon to see face to face, and to love and enjoy forever. He preferred often to be left alone, that he might the more freely indulge his pious feelings, and for this end he would allow no one to watch by him at night, until his mortal agony had begun. When his friends affectionately sought to know what they could do to relieve his sufferings, he would answer them by pointing out some passage of Sacred Scripture, or chapter of the 'Following of Christ,' which he desired them to read to him, or by asking them to say some prayers for his happy death. No agonies of pain could extort from him a single expression of distress. 'The will of God be done,' was the constant language of his lips, as it was the abiding sentiment of his heart.

"When preparing to receive the Holy Viaticum, he wrote to us in the true spirit of saintly humility requesting the prayers of our seminary and of the sisterhood, and begging pardon for whatever offences or bad example he had ever given to any one at either institution. A few days before his dissolution, the strength of his naturally vigorous constitution rallied for a time, and his physician promised him at least a temporary recovery: he told the physician he was mistaken, and whether he knew it supernaturally or otherwise, named the exact time of his approaching departure. He gave himself the orders for preparing his grave, and as calmly directed the modes of sepulture, and proper rites to be observed, as if he was discharging an ordinary duty. On the morning of the day before his death, he remarked to the clergyman, who attended him with unwearied solicitude and affection: 'My dear child, I have the whole day yet to stay with you, to-morrow with God!' To another pious friend, he used these simple but expressive words: 'I am going home.'

"Heaven was indeed his home: He had always so regarded it; there was his treasure; his heart was there; he had ever longed to be with God, and 'see Him as He is'; and now the door of the Father's House was opening to him, and Angels were on the wing to meet his departing spirit, and conduct it to its place of rest. He was happy therefore amid the pangs and terrors of death; for he trusted that he was but going home. After having received the last sacrament, he directed the departing prayers to be recited, which he answered devoutly and fervently until the last, and then on the morning of the 26th of June, at half past one o'clock, he calmly and sweetly surrendered his soul into the hands of his Creator.

"His death was deplored as a general calamity. He was especially lamented by the poor, the widow and orphan. The people of Vincennes felt that they had lost a public benefactor, and his own flock both clergy and laity bewailed, as well they might, the death of such a pastor. All, with one accord, mourned for the scholar, the philanthropist and the saint. Crowds of persons of every rank, and of all denominations, visited his corpse, and assisted at the ceremonies of his burial. The mayor and civil authorities, and learned societies of Vincennes, passed resolutions to attend his funeral. The whole population poured forth to accompany, in solemn silence, his honored remains to their last resting place on earth."

According to the custom, his body was buried under the

sanctuary of his cathedral. The memory of "good Bishop Bruté," as he is always called, has not been dimmed by time. Those who knew him and who were trained to virtue by his precepts and example, love to speak of him, to repeat his words, and to tell the incidents of his saintly life. In consequence, of all the holy missionaries whom God has from time to time sent to plant the seeds of faith in this new country, no name is more often repeated, no labours are more often dwelt upon, than his—and thus, the undying influence of his beautiful example still helps on the good cause to which his life was devoted—the salvation of souls, and the greater glory of God.

INDEX

OTHER BOOKS FROM OUR SUNDAY VISITOR

RELIGION FOR LITTLE CHILDREN: A Parents' Guide

By Christiane Brusselmans, Ph.D. in Religious Education, with Edward Wakin, *cloth* $4.95, *paper* $2.95

Informative, heart warming chapters which include Preparing for Baptism, Family Prayer, A Child's Sunday, A Child's Christmas, The Special Role of Grandparents, and more. It has a section devoted to the 76 questions most asked by children, with the answers. Must reading for parents and educators.

HAPPINESS OVER THE HILL

By Rev. Joseph E. Manton, C.SS.R., *cloth* $4.95, *paper* $1.95

Reflections for everyday Christian living. Stories of saints and sinners and situations. Thoughts about our Lord and our Lady.

WHAT CATHOLICS BELIEVE TODAY

By Msgr. Paul Poupard, *paper* 95¢

Addressed to all those who are baptized and intended to help them know the Catholic Faith better. Soul-searching writings on The Mystery of God, The Joy of Believing, On the Way to Eternity, Hope, and more. Includes Pope Paul VI's Prayer for Faith.

THE CATHOLIC RELIGION

By Most Rev. Bernard D. Stewart, Bishop of Sandhurst, Australia, *paper* $1.25

An outline of Catholic doctrine from statements made by Pope Paul VI and by Vatican Council II concerning fundamental truths of the Catholic Religion. The table of contents are very complete. Included are the corrections to be made to the New Dutch Catechism and answers suggested to some current questions raised in lectures on religious doctrine.

If your bookseller does not have these titles, you may order them by sending listed price (we pay postage and handling) to the Book Department at the address below. Enclose check or money order — do not send cash.

Write for free book list

Our Sunday Visitor, Inc. / Noll Plaza / Huntington, Ind. 46750